Women and Public Administration: International Perspectives

Women and Public Administration: International Perspectives

Jane H. Bayes
Editor

Women and Public Administration: International Perspectives, edited by Jane H. Bayes, was simultaneously issued by The Haworth Press, Inc., under the same title, as special issue of the journal *Women & Politics*, Volume 11, Number 4, 1991, Rita Mae Kelly, Editor.

Harrington Park Press
An Imprint of
The Haworth Press, Inc.
New York • London • Sydney

ISBN 1-56023-014-2

Published by

Harrington Park Press, 10 Alice Street, Binghamton, NY 13904-1580
EUROSPAN/Harrington, 3 Henrietta Street, London WC2E 8LU England
ASTAM/Harrington, 162-168 Parramatta Road, Stanmore, Sydney, N.S.W. 2048 Australia

Harrington Park Press is an imprint of The Haworth Press, Inc., 10 Alice Street, Binghamton, NY 13904-1580.

Women and Public Administration: International Perspectives was originally published as *Women & Politics*, Volume 11, Number 4 1991.

Library of Congress Cataloging-in-Publication Data

Women and public administration : international perspectives / Jane H. Bayes, editor.
　　p. cm.
　　"Originally published as Women & politics, volume 11, number 4 1991"—T.p. verso.
　　ISBN 1-56023-014-2 (acid free paper)
　　1. Women in the civil service. I. Bayes, Jane H., 1939- .
JF1601.W66 1991
351.1′0082—dc20
91-36589
CIP

CONTENTS

ABOUT THE EDITOR

JANE H. BAYES is Professor and Chair of the Department of Political Science at California State University, Northridge. She is currently serving as Chair of the Sex Roles and Politics Research Committee of the International Political Science Association for 1988-1991. She is author of *Minority Politics and Ideologies in the United States* (Chandler and Sharp 1982), *Ideologies and Interest Group Politics* (Chandler and Sharp 1982), and co-edited *Comparable Worth, Pay Equity, and Public Policy* with Rita Mae Kelly (Greenwood Press 1988). Her research interests include women and politics, political economy, and minority politics.

SYMPOSIUM

Women in Public Administration:
A Comparative Perspective —
Introduction

Jane H. Bayes
Jeanne Marie Col

THE ORIGINS OF THIS STUDY

This symposium is the product of an international research project begun in 1982 by Jeanne Marie Col at the International Political Science
Association in Rio de Janeiro, Brazil. The initial purpose was to provide a
global report on the status of women in public administration for the end
of the United Nations' Decade of Women meeting in Nairobi, Kenya in
1985. This goal was accomplished in rudimentary form in a progress report delivered at the Nairobi meeting. Once begun, the project raised
questions and opportunities for comparison that went well beyond its initial conception. Researchers met in Paris, France in 1985 and in Bonn,
Germany in 1986 to share their results. These meetings brought to light a
wealth of data about women in public administration throughout the
world. Having a project where as many as twenty different researchers
from almost as many countries and from all continents met for three days
to share and compare their findings on the topic of women in public administration was an extremely exhilarating experience. The rewards and
the insights, as well as the difficulties and frustrations of designing and

1

completing a cooperative international research project became apparent to all. Perhaps as important as the outcome of the project has been the process that it represents.

The first planning meeting for the project was in Groningen, Netherlands at the Second International Interdisciplinary Congress on Women in 1984. Jeanne Marie Col had been working extensively on a series of United Nations workshops and projects dedicated to training women in public administration in developing nations. The initial questions that she proposed to the Sex Roles and Politics Research Committee of the International Political Science Association concerned identifying and documenting barriers to the entry and advancement of women in public administration in various countries in the world. These barriers involved sex role socialization processes, sex role stereotyping on the job, access to education for women, entry level barriers, and promotion practices. For four intense days in Groningen, a group of about ten researchers from almost as many countries met in a hotel room to plan a research design. This included designing a questionnaire and an interview schedule. The participants were extremely aware of cultural differences and of the various meanings of terms and concepts in different languages and cultures. (All participants spoke English, although English was the native language of only three or four.) Comparing countries of such disparate size and complexity as Bulgaria (4.6 million) and India (685 million) brought home the limitations of the need to use nation states and/or governments as the basic comparative unit in a project on public administration. The group was very sensitive to the dangers of imposing a Western model on non-western countries in these discussions, yet all participants shared certain general Western liberal assumptions about public bureaucracies and their political importance in political decision-making as well as assumptions concerning the need for women to be a part of that decision-making process at the highest levels.

THE GENERAL POSITION OF WOMEN
IN THE LABOR FORCE

The participants' ideas concerning a comparative framework for the study involved placing the discussion of women in public administration in the context of women's overall participation in the labor force of each country. The general hypothesis was that public sector employment has led women's advancement into higher status jobs. For socialist countries where all employment may be considered public, the initial assumption was that economic control by the state opened new opportunities for women. In developing nations, the assumption was that the labor force participation by women would help define the extent to which the country's female population was rural versus urban, agricultural versus manufacturing or service oriented, and give a rough index of women's education levels. This, in turn, would set the parameters for assessing women's opportunities in public administration.

In addition to the overall context of women in the labor force, the researchers chose to focus on four other topics: (1) a general description of the number and level of female civil servants in the highest ranks of at least two bureaucracies, one concerned with traditionally female roles such as health or education, and one concerned with traditionally male roles such as finance; (2) the career histories of these women; (3) an institutional description of women in public bureaucracies, women's views of the barriers, the obstacles, the access to training and advancement, and the general social climate for women employees at various levels within the bureaucracies in question. The research design sought to obtain information about how women in high level positions performed in the workplace and what their attitudes were about their own positions in their organizations, their work styles, and their attitudes towards both men and women superiors and subordinates. Finally, (4) the study probed the perceptions of women in public administration concerning discrimination and equality policies. Each of these topics deserves some elaboration.

A GENERAL DESCRIPTION OF WOMEN IN TOP ADMINISTRATIVE POSITIONS

An original hypothesis of the research design was that ministries would exhibit occupational sex segregation according to the extent to which their functions had traditionally been associated with one sex or the other. The unknown question was the extent to which this pattern prevailed. Also of interest was the percentage of women who were "top" bureaucrats in each country. Defining a "top" bureaucrat presented some interesting comparative methodological problems. Each researcher was to examine female executives in the top ten percent of the salary range for her country. This rule created a number of methodological dilemmas especially in small countries where very few if any women were in top positions in traditionally male dominated bureaucracies such as those concerned with finance or foreign affairs. After documenting the number and status of women in the top ranks of the bureaucracy of each country, the research design called for each researcher to identify a sample of at least 25 top female bureaucrats (and if possible, 25 top male bureaucrats) as question-naire recipients and as candidates for an interview.

The Career Histories
of The Women Administrators

The purpose of exploring the career histories of the respondents was to identify and document socialization and recruitment patterns as well as barriers which these women had confronted and overcome. Were career paths for women different from those of men? Were women limited to top positions in certain ministries and excluded from others? Did successful women tend to move laterally more than successful men? Did women move around from one agency to another or from one job to another more often than did men as they advanced? Did a "glass ceiling" seem to be in evidence for women administrators? Were the respondents "pioneer" women in the agency or had the agency or ministry a history of women in top administrative positions? What were the class and educational back-grounds of the top administrative women? Would these be different in different countries?

Hypothesized Barriers to Women
Interested in Public Administration Careers

The existing literature about the status of women in practically every society suggests that in all the nations of the world, women interested in public administration as a career will have to cope with common barriers. These include socialization practices that teach women that they should not aspire to such positions in society and continue to reiterate this mes-sage in countless aspects of everyday life; the sex segregation of occupa-tions in the society and sex role stereotyping on the job; the lack of access to education or training in general or in particular fields; and entry level barriers. Once on the job, promotion practices often present barriers, and finally the double burden of family and career affects even those women who are not mothers because of sex role stereotyping. The assumption was that these barriers are present to some degree in all societies although their prevalence varies.

Sex Role Socialization

Early childhood socialization trains girls and boys for future roles in society. Except in relatively rare cases, children are trained to assume the roles with which their parents are comfortable, rather than roles based on changing needs and conditions. While boys are expected to emphasize

CQ

public roles, girls are trained in household duties and discouraged from public activities. The stereotype of the passive, feminine, family oriented wife-mother is re-learned by each generation and reinforced daily through schooling, customs, institutions, laws, and the media. Even though there are many women who choose other behavior patterns, these non-traditional women experience role-incongruence, role stress, and role conflict. The researchers were concerned with the extent to which this sex role socialization occurred for top female bureaucrats.

Sex Role Stereotyping on the Job

Practically all societies have some kind of sex-based division of labor, although the extent of the separation and isolation of women varies considerably from one country to another. Stereotypes concerning appropriate behavior for women will vary accordingly. Where women are pioneering by assuming managerial and top administrative positions, they are challenging by their very existence long held expectations and stereotypes. Many women, as well as men, prefer not to be the "first" pioneer in developing new careers, new fields, or new roles. The psychological, social, and even economic challenges are many for those women and men who seek innovative roles. A woman who chooses to fill a position previously filled only by men must invent, test, and refine behavior patterns in entirely new situations, knowing that her colleagues are watching to see whether she will try to be "one of the boys" or will attempt to alter their expectations about behavior associated with that position. Role models become extremely important here. An individual looks for one or more persons who have similar personal characteristics and who are already in positions similar to those to which the individual aspires. Upwardly mobile men have plenty of examples of men at higher levels and can easily identify with at least a few of them. Pioneering women, however, can find few if any women who are already highly placed in most organizations. At best, an entry level woman finds one or two women at higher levels. She may or may not identify with their role behaviors. Only when a number of women hold high positions in many organizations will entry level women have enough potential role models to find models whose abilities and styles they admire. The lack of female role models in top organizational positions broadcasts a "no entrance" signal to the most qualified and interested women. While some women do respond adventurously, men do not have this additional barrier to confront. Once roles have been de-stereotyped sexually, both men and women will pursue careers based on their abilities and inclinations, rather than following the paths taken most often by members of their sex. The extent to which top female bureaucrats actually were pioneers and the ways in which they experienced the pioneering role were questions of concern to the researchers.

Being the only or one of very few highly placed women in an organization brings with it a number of problems which male leaders in those organizations do not have to face. Isolation is one of these. Most leadership positions are filled by men who are used to relating to women as mother, sister, daughter, or secretary-assistant. Many professional males have never worked with a female colleague. The "token" woman in a top management position consequently must work not only to develop her own style, but must also work to make her male colleagues comfortable with her. She must spend extra effort to communicate with her male colleagues and to be included in their informal activities and discussions. As one or one of a few highly placed women, she is not only isolated but she is also very visible and constantly being watched. Whereas most men entering a job can make a few mistakes that are overlooked, a woman in the same position is under great pressure to perform well every minute. If she makes a mistake, her male colleagues may infer that "women" are inappropriate for the job. If she does well, they are just as likely to conclude that she is exceptional and that most women could not do as well. In the first case, she reflects poorly on the entire group of potential female employees; if she does well, she is separated from "expectations" about women and becomes isolated from her female cohort. The interview schedule attempted to probe how "pioneering" respondents perceived themselves and their job situation in light of these hypotheses.

Still another barrier to advancement for women comes from the disjunction between the passive socialization training for women in most societies and the requirements for advancement that most organizations present. While qualified women do not automatically get the top jobs, they are more likely to be promoted if they express ambition, seek difficult assignments, and speak out on issues. Supervisors who do not consider themselves to be biased against women may still treat women differently from men because of their own expectations concerning women's ambitions and desires for advancement. Supervisors may (sometimes unintentionally) exclude women employees from developmental opportunities such as travel and attendance at conferences, exclude them from professional networks, pass over women employees when doling out important and difficult assignments, and confine women to secondary or assistant helpmate roles. Worse, women may be treated in a domineering or condescending manner, overprotected or constantly criticized, or subjected to harassment. An ambitious woman must not only do her job well, she must confront any internal reluctance she may have to be aggressive in seeking choice assignments and responsibilities, and must consume additional energy developing strategies to deal with any prejudices her male supervisors and colleagues may have. All of these ideas were hypotheses that the research team sought to test in their interviewing.

ACCESS TO EDUCATION

While most developed countries offer universal access to primary education (although the quality varies from place to place), in many developing countries, one must pay for access to a limited number of spaces, even at the lowest levels. Parental attitudes influence whether girls have the same educational opportunities as boys. Enrollment in formal education for women of all age groups lags behind that of men, but is increasing at a faster rate than for men.

Lack of parental resources and traditional attitudes limit the educational opportunities for many women. For less wealthy families, the cost of sending children to school may require parents to choose among their children. In developing countries, parents send boys instead of girls because girls are expected to be mothers, not providers, and because girls can get pregnant and be forced to leave school. In industrialized countries, the same considerations operate at a higher level of education. Boys are the first to be sent to college in a family that has to choose. Only within the last twenty years in industrialized nations have women obtained access to training in any great numbers in traditionally "male" fields such as engineering, science, medicine, business, law, economics, and politics. In many of these fields in many countries, education and training is still primarily for males. The research project probed respondents concerning their education and the support they received in obtaining that education.

ENTRY LEVEL BARRIERS
INTO PUBLIC SERVICE

Occupational sex segregation represents a significant barrier to women's advancement in practically every country. The expectation of those engaged in this study was that traditionally "male" ministries such as those dealing with finance and foreign affairs would have fewer women in high positions than ministries concerned with typically "female" functions, such as health, social welfare, and education. In countries where trained labor is plentiful, educated women may experience more discrimination than in countries where educated labor is scarce and the possession of knowledge and skills is considered a national resource not to be wasted by systematically underutilizing women graduates.

PROMOTION

Higher level performance (and usually higher salaries) is related to the following job characteristics: (a) supervising more people; (b) responsibility for a larger budget or more expensive equipment; (c) handling tasks in which errors have more serious consequences for the organization; (d) responsibility for making decisions for which there are fewer precedents and for which outcomes are harder to predict; (e) handling tasks that require coordination of more independent agencies or more different types of employees or clients. An upwardly mobile employee looks for opportunities either (1) to step into a position with the above characteristics or (2) to alter the current job to include more of the above characteristics.

A major barrier to promotion for women comes from the specificity of job titles and the lock-step sequencing of positions into career ladders and regulations limiting movement among agencies. If women are blocked from entering the lowest levels of such career ladders they are automatically excluded from promotion into higher positions on those ladders. Career ladders dominated by women are short and have low starting salaries in comparison with those career ladders dominated by men that are taller and have higher salaries. If job titles were broad-banded and more job titles were interchangeable, women could more easily change from a short to a taller career ladder. Some government agencies have developed "bridge jobs" that span two career ladders and increase lateral mobility across career ladders. In each country, researchers were looking for evidence of career ladders and how they affected women as well as for the existence of policies or practices that attempted to include more women in such career ladders.

Employee evaluation practices present another structural barrier to women's promotability. Evaluation systems often weight subjective factors such as personality and appearance criteria where such weighting is inappropriate. Because women are rarely found in managerial positions, evaluators are not sure whether behavior and accomplishments that they observe are due to the woman's true abilities or to the fact that she is a woman. For example, if a man is often seen talking with other employees, this may be interpreted as an expression of his interpersonal skills. If a woman talks to other employees in the same way, she may be viewed as gossiping and wasting time. Although the behavior is the same, the interpretation is different for women and men. If a supervisor of a woman employee has strong "traditional" attitudes about women's place and about women's behavior, the supervisor may see negative behavior even when the woman is doing very well.

Many behaviors towards women in an organization are hostile whether intentional or subconsciously motivated. Women managers may be singled out, either by being ignored or by being made to feel special or different. A lone woman in a meeting is often asked for the women's point of view. This may appear conciliatory or sensitive but may be a device to set her apart from the group. Managers not knowing how to relate to a female manager may set her apart by avoiding eye contact, by maintaining more physical distance, and by making references to her femininity.

A number of male behavioral patterns are condescending. These not only distance women from the management team but also place women at the lowest levels of the status hierarchy. These behaviors include: non-parallel terminology (e.g., men and "girls"); obvious surprise when a woman does well; a "knowing" smile when a woman does not do well; non-parallel titles (e.g., *Mr. Khan* and *Leila*); the inability to remember names and professional attributes and accomplishments of women (while remembering very well their physical appearance); and a lack of interest in women managers as potentially powerful and long term components of the organization.

Some behaviors are not only condescending but also domineering: making inappropriate personal remarks; belittling or ignoring suggestions made by women; attributing comments made by women to men instead; supervising women professionals more closely than men; using sexist humor to enliven speeches or conversations; and seeking analysis (higher level information) from men while seeking facts (lower level information) from women. In conferences and meetings, men, rather than women, tend to talk more, talk longer, take more turns speaking, exert more control over the topic of conversation, and interrupt women more often than men. These micro-inequalities taken singly are merely irritating, but when a woman is subjected repeatedly to these condescending and domineering behaviors, any doubts she has about her abilities and performance are reinforced. Such negative behaviors can discourage a woman from taking the initiative, suggesting ideas, and developing professional relationships. Her aspirations are dampened and her confidence undermined. The questionnaire asked respondents for their views on promotion practices in light of the above hypotheses.

THE PLAN OF THIS SYMPOSIUM

Each of the papers in this symposium begins with a discussion of women in the labor force as a means of establishing the context for women in the top public administrative jobs in each country. Some papers also include some historical, demographic, economic, and governmental information about the country as background material. Each paper then briefly describes the structure of state administration and the peculiarities of the research design as it was executed in each country. The researchers in each country all used the same questionnaire and interview schedule. The data reported here may not appear exactly parallel in that sampling procedures varied in each country and the brief reports presented here emphasize the findings which each researcher found to be most significant. These varied from country to country.

In the case studies that follow, the authors, all of whom were born and currently live in the country about which they write, report a rather dismal situation for those who would hope to see equality between men and women in public administration leadership positions. On the other hand, change for women has been taking place rapidly in all of the societies and in the situation for women in general, and for top women administrators in particular, today is better than it has been in the past. In all countries except India, women have entered the paid work force in ever greater numbers during the last two decades, especially in professional managerial and service occupations. In all of the countries, the public sector has been an important source of employment for women; however, women have only been able to occupy between 1-5 percent of the top administrative positions if viewed as a whole. In a few top national ministries, women hold as many as 16 percent of the top positions.

In addition to documenting the status of women in top administrative positions in each country, the case studies discuss the barriers to women's advancement as they manifest themselves in each country. The situation in each country has its own unique story involving history, the structure of the labor market, the organization of government in the country, the socialization patterns of the culture as well as the current patterns of interaction between men and women, and current public policies affecting these matters. These circumstances help to define the reported objective barriers to women's advancement in public administration in each country as well as the subjective attitudes and behaviors that the women respondents themselves report in each case study.

SIMILARITIES AND DIFFERENCES:
A WORD OF WARNING

Reported similarities often mask substantial differences. For example, all of the women interviewed for these studies were highly educated with the minimum of a university degree and often with an advanced degree. This "fact" can have very different meanings in different countries. In countries where primary education is not universal, as in India, this means that recruitment into public service is possible only for the more privileged upper classes. The higher education of the Indian women administrators involves quite a different economic, and social process for the society than does the higher education of women in the United States, Finland, or Bulgaria.

In all the countries, public administration jobs tend to be sex segregated, although in varying degrees. Sinkkonen and Hänninen-Salmelin explain that in Finland, the very levels of government are sex segregated as traditionally female government services are administered at the local level primarily by women, and traditionally male dominated government services like foreign affairs and finance occur at the national level and have males in the top jobs. No other country in this study is administered in quite this sex segregated way.

In all countries, women continue to have primary responsibility for childcare, a problem which many top women administrators attempt to resolve either by not having children, by having fewer children than the rest of the population, or by engaging in part-time work. In all countries, role conflict and often the double burden of career and family is intensely felt by top female administrators. However, variations occur. Leyenaar describes the "culture of motherhood" that characterizes the climate women live in in the Netherlands. She explains the causes and the consequences of this "culture" for women in top administrative positions.

Sometimes specific or unique legal, administrative, or cultural practices have prevented women from gaining top administrative jobs. The paper on Finland explains that although Finland was the second nation in the world to give women the vote as early as 1906, Finnish women have been prevented from holding certain top administrative jobs in certain areas in the recent past because statutes specifically stated that these jobs could not be filled by women. In the Federal Republic of Germany chapter, Langkau-Herrmann and Sessar-Karpp note that German women cannot gain entry to certain ministries because they lack the required graduate degrees in economics or law, educational areas where women have historically been underrepresented.

An underlying, although not consciously articulated assumption of the initial research design for this study was that top administrative positions generally are associated with political power and that women desire such positions just as men do. The case studies that follow show, however, that job satisfaction is not the same for top women administrators in each country. Women in the United States and in the Federal Republic of Germany were highly satisfied with their jobs, whereas Ananieva and Razvigorova and Swarup and Sinha found that for different reasons top women administrators in Bulgaria and India were less satisfied.

The chapters that follow present the particular situation for women in public administration in each country included in this symposium. In the final chapter, Bayes compares the data gathered in each country with regard to the initial questions posed by all the researchers and then highlights some of the substantial differences between the countries in the symposium and the barriers these countries present to women in public administration. The argument is that some major factors such as the nature of the economy (agricultural, industrializing, industrial, or post-industrial), the structure of the labor force, the role of the state in the economy and in the society, and the availability of education in the society are characteristics which establish some of the parameters for women's role in society and specifically for women's role in high levels of public administration. States that are primarily agricultural, largely rural, and which have high levels of illiteracy, as does India, treat women and women administrators differently than do states that are industrial, mostly urban, and which exhibit low levels of illiteracy. States like Bulgaria, that are centrally directed, interested in rapid modernization, or have a need for skilled or highly educated labor, are more inclined to draw women into a wider range of roles than states which exhibit none of these characteristics. Beyond generalizations such as these, the stories of the barriers that women face in becoming top public administrators, and the stories of what it is like to be a woman in a top administrative post in any particular country are different for every country. Similarities exist and are instructive to note; however, these similarities may be generated by quite different conditions.

Women in Public Administration in India

Hem Lata Swarup
Niroj Sinha

BACKGROUND

India, with a female population of 330,786,808 out of a total of 685,184,692, according to the 1981 Census of India (Padmanabh 1983), is the second biggest country in terms of female population. However, the status of Indian women in all spheres of their lives, socio-economic, political, and cultural, has been secondary to the status of males. The 1971 Census revealed shocking statistics about the conditions of women in India. Although the literacy percentage for women had increased from 13 percent to 18.7 percent during the decade, the work participation rate had declined steeply from 27.9 percent to 12.1 percent. In response to the census findings, the government established The Status of Women Committee to investigate and report on the status of Indian women. In 1974 the committee submitted its report which called for measures to improve the situation of women in all spheres.

Reformers such as Raja Ram Mohan Roy, Keshavchandra Sen, Swami Dayan and Saraswati called for improvement in the socio-economic conditions of women in the nineteenth century. They made efforts to educate women, prohibit the system of child-marriage, and eliminate widow burning (Sati) with the help of the government. The result was a massive upsurge of women in the national freedom struggle under the guidance of Mahatma Gandhi and Nehru. Gandhi and Nehru had recognized the potential of women and their possible participation in the social and political life of the nation. Important changes did take place in pre-Independence India, changes which received further impetus in Independent India. The changes included:

- the spread of education among women;
- the prohibition of such social evils as the practice of child marriage, widow burning and female infanticide;
- the inclusion of women on a mass scale in the national freedom struggle from 1920 onwards;
- the guarantee of equal social-economic and political rights by the Constitution of Independent India;
- the spread of employment opportunities.

Changes in the social structure, such as the breakdown of the joint family system and the emergence of nuclear family units, a certain degree of urbanization, and the entry of men and women into the service segment of the economy, have helped to change the lives of a minority of Indian women. For the majority, life has not changed much.

WOMEN IN THE LABOR FORCE

The female participation rate in the labor force declined from 41.8 million (34.4 percent) in 1911 to 31.2 million (17.4 percent) in 1971, with 87 percent of this female labor concentrated primarily in rural areas. Of the total female labor force, 80 percent is in agriculture. Within the two categories of agricultural labor, the number of female cultivators declined from 45.4 percent in 1951 to 29.6 percent in 1971, but then increased to 33.2 percent in 1981. During this same period, the number of women who have worked as agricultural laborers has increased from 31.4 percent in 1951 to 50.5 percent in 1971, and then declined slightly to 46.2 percent in 1981. Female participation in industry declined from 11.4 percent in 1951 to 8.7 percent in 1972 (Guha 1975, 163). Increased participation for women has come only in the services and professions where it increased from 28,000 in 1961 to 1.3 million in 1975 in the public sector.

Most women are concentrated in Class III or clerical level jobs. In the professions, most women are teachers. Of all teachers in India, 70 percent are women. Of these, 71 percent are engaged in primary school teaching and only 8 percent in college teaching. In medicine, the ratio is 6.1 females to every 100 male doctors. Seventy percent of all nurses are women. The number of female administrators, directors, managers, and executives, which are the highest ranked occupations in the country, increased from 49,000 to 54,000 during the decade 1961-1971. The comparable growth for men was from 1,962,000 to 2,586,000 (Mitra 1980). In spite of the slight increase in this occupational group, the subcategory of women administrators and executive officials in the government declined from 17,000 to 14,000 while the number of male administrators and executive officials rose from 1,014,000 to 1,528,000.

Women's employment has continued to grow in the service sector although the Census of 1981 reports that women's employment declined in agriculture and industry. The public sector has been increasingly providing employment for women in comparison with the private sector. The figures show that 47.1 percent of women's employment was in the public sector in 1972-73. By 1976-77, this figure had increased to 52 percent (Table 1). Much of this increase has come at the state level. During the same period, women's percentage of the total labor force increased from 21.4 percent to 24.9 percent (Reserve Bank of India 1978). The relatively low level of participation by women in all employment sectors is due to a number of factors:

- protective labor laws, such as the Factories Act of 1952, the Plantation and Labor Act of 1951, and the Maternity Benefits Acts of 1961;
- illiteracy, lack of skill, lack of occupational mobility among women in agricultural labor. The literacy ratio according to the 1981 Census is 24.82 percent of females compared to 46.89 percent for males;
- the rigid hold of social norms on middle class, semi-educated women to remain in their homes and play the role of wife and mother only;
- the lack of child-care centers, the lack of electrical gadgets to simplify housework, the unavailability of cooked food at reasonable prices.

Sexual stereotyping is the major issue for female labor participation. Jobs have been classified into male/female categories by the National Employment Service. The Vocational Training facilities discriminate against women. Of the total number of trainees, only 4 percent are women. Wage discrimination is widespread. The wage boards fix wages according to sex in private industry and in the unorganized sector of agriculture, women usually receive lower wages for equal amounts of work.

Although the participation rate is low, the percentage of unemployed women when compared to men is quite high. In 1971, the total number of unemployed women in rural areas was 2.1 million compared to 1.4 million men. In agriculture, women formed 60 percent of the total unemployed, according to the Committee on Unemployment. Women, on an average, have fewer paid working days (160 days) in comparison to men (242 days). The proportion of highly educated and professionally unemployed women is nearly 41 percent among female graduates in the arts and

Table 1

<u>Trends in Women's Employment</u>

End March	Total Employment	%Women of Total	% of Women's Employment by Sector	
			Public	Private
1972-73	1,882,400	21.35	47.1	52.9
1973-74	1,927,900	21.88	49.2	50.8
1974-75	1,967,200	22.31	50.6	49.4
1975-76	2,020,800	23.97	50.9	49.1
1976-77	2,071,600	24.94	52.0	48.0

Source: Reserve Bank of India Bulletin, October, 1978.

humanities. In 1971, only 6 female doctors were employed for every 100 male doctors.

WOMEN IN PUBLIC ADMINISTRATION

Since Independence in 1947, the Constitution has permitted Indian women to enter the administrative services, especially in the public sector. During the British rule, women were disqualified for higher administrative posts. Immediately after Independence, women were allowed to take the competitive examination for the administrative service. However, rule 5(3) of the Indian Administrative Services' Rules of 1954 empowered the government to demand the resignation of a female officer after marriage on grounds of efficiency. After women parliamentarians and women leaders raised a hue and cry against this provision, the I.A.S. deleted it from their recruitment rules in 1972. Nevertheless, the percentage of women remains very low — not more than 11 percent of the total.

The governmental administrative structure in India consists of three general categories: Central Services, State Services, and Local Government Services. Within the Central Services are four classes: Class I includes the Indian Administrative Services (I.A.S.), the Indian Foreign Service (I.F.S.), the Indian Police Service (I.P.S.), and Allied Services. Class II includes officers at the section office level; Class III consists of clerical and ministerial cadre services; and Class IV involves peons, sweepers, and other unskilled labor. The State Services also have four classes in the same pattern as the central government. Class I includes provincial civil, police, education, and other services. The Local Government Services involve metropolitan areas, corporations, municipalities, district boards and panchayats at the village level.

Table 2 shows the trend of women's employment in the central government at different levels from 1961 to 1971. The largest number of women are concentrated in Class III jobs. The expansion in this cadre has been faster than in others—from 720 in 1961 to 4,175 in 1971 (Guha 1975, 209). The trend has continued although detailed data is not available.

Women in Central Services:
The Indian Administrative Services (I.A.S.)

Women started entering this most prestigious of the Indian Services in 1951. Apart from the Indian Administrative, Foreign and Police Services, women were also entering the private sector as directors, managers, and executives of financial and commercial corporations and industrial establishments during this period. In the first decade (1950-1960), the number of women rarely exceeded 4 percent in any one year, and that was only at the end of the decade. During the second decade, women began to participate in greater numbers with the percentage of women hovering around

Table 2

Women Employed in Central Government at Different Levels

(Class I is the highest)

Level		Class I 1961	1971	Class II 1961	1971	Class III 1961	1971	Class IV 1961	1971
General	#	29	176	267	785	549	2,959	5	68
	%	(69)	(70)	(95)	(90)	(76)	(71)	(50)	(81)
Technical	#	7	29	13	61	109	902	2	8
	%	(17)	(12)	(4)	(7)	(15)	(22)	(20)	(10)
Professional	#	6	46	1	23	62	314	3	8
	%	(14)	(18)	(1)	(3)	(9)	(8)	(3)	(10)
Total Women	#	42	215	231	269	720	4,175	10	84
	%	(100)	(100)	(100)	(100)	(100)	(101)	(100)	(101)

Figures in brackets denote percentages.
Source: Guha, 1975.

10-13 percent. In 1969, the contingent of women selected was 18.29 percent (15 out of a total of 82), the largest in two decades. The number of selected women ranged from 1 to 15, with 10 women being selected in 1966, 1967, and 1970.

The third decade began with the appointment of a Committee on the Status of Women in India (CSWI). The numbers and proportions of women began to increase. During the decade, the percentage of women selected for the I.A.S ranged from 7 to 20 percent of the total. Except for 1978, women's percentage of the total did not fall below 10 percent. For four years women recruits constituted 15 percent of the total and during two of the years, the recruitment figures for women were nearly 20 percent of the total.

During the 1980s decade, the first four years did not display spectacular results. The number of female recruits to the I.A.S. ranged from 11 to 16 women in any one year and in percentage constitutes from 8 to 10 percent of the total. This represents a decline in the growth of women in the Indian Central Services. The promising increase in the numbers of women in the Central Services during the 1970s was not maintained during the 1980s.

Recruitment and promotion. Besides direct recruitment, other methods of entry into the I.A.S. include special recruitments, recruitments based on released examination results, and promotion from State Services or Provincial Civil Services (P.C.S.) (see Table 3). Between 1948 and 1983, 9.2 percent of the 3,215 direct recruits into the I.A.S. were female. Of the 955 promoted during that period, only 6 were female. All special recruits, numbering 75 from 1948 to 1971, and all those recruited from released examination results, numbering 90 from 1966 to 1973, were male (Department of Personnel and Administrative Reforms 1984). The same pattern appears in the other top services of the nation.

Some of the states have recruited a greater percentage of women I.A.S. officers than others. Himanchal Pradesh has the highest percentage with 16.4 percent. Union Territories (15.3 percent), Haryana (15.3 percent), Punjab (14.8 percent), Tamilnadu (12.8 percent) and Karnataka (10.6 percent) all follow. All other states have recruited fewer than 10 percent women I.A.S. officers. The states of Assam, Meghalaya, Tripura, Manipur, Jammu and Kashmir, Orissa and Sikkim all have less than 5 percent women I.A.S. officers. All of these states, except Orissa, have had problems of integration with the Central Government at one time or another and have yet to become a part of the mainstream. The Hindi heartland performs poorly in this arena also, as it does in other spheres. A correlation seems to exist between lower percentages of female I.A.S. officers and general socio-economic backwardness.

Table 3

Direct Recruitment and Promotion to Indian Administrative Service (I.A.S.)

Mode of Recruitment	Total	Men	Women	% Women to Total
Direct Recruitment to I.A.S. from 1948-1983	3,214	2,918	297	9.23
Special Recruitment various schemes 1948-1971	75	75	1	1.31
Released Examination Results 1966-1973	90	90	-	-
Promotion Quota	955	949	6	0.62
Total	4,336	4,032	304	7.01

Source: Department of Personnel and Administrative Reforms, 1984.

The structure of pay scales and career advancement. The pay structure of the I.A.S. and other services as fixed by the Government of India, which constitutionally cannot discriminate overtly between men and women, was revised in 1973 in accordance with the Pay Commission Report, Appendix III:

- Junior Scale — Rs. 700-1300 with efficiency bar after Rs. 800
- Senior Scale — Rs. 1200-2000
- Selection Grade — Rs. 2000-2250
- Supertime Scale
    i. Rs. 2500-2750
    ii. Rs. 3000-Fixed
    iii. Rs. 3500-Fixed

An I.A.S. officer can qualify for the supertime scale of Rs. 2500-2750 after 16 or 18 years of experience. These are the posts of commissioners and secretaries to state governments. At the central government level, officers of this rank, if deputized to the Government of India, hold Joint Secretary rank. The scale of Rs. 3000-fixed is open to officers at the level of Additional Secretary to the Government of India and Member of Boards of Revenue in the states. The Rs. 3500-fixed pay rate is for the Secretaries to the Government of India, Chief Secretaries of the State Governments and the Chairman of the Board of Revenue in each State. Only the post of Cabinet Secretary (Chief Secretary to the Government of India) is higher in the Supertime scale. This is a political appointment and has never been held by a woman. In 1985 for the first time, the highest ranking I.A.S. woman was appointed to the post of Principal Secretary to the Prime Minister. She continued to hold this post in 1988. As Table 4 shows the percentages of women in the top levels of the I.A.S. at the Selection Grade and above in both the central and in the state administrations ranged from about 3 to 7 percent of the total (see Tables 4 and 5).

The overall picture for the position of women in public administration in India is not very bright. Women have never been able to obtain more than 11 percent of the positions in the Indian Administrative Service. In 1984, only 311 of the total 3,349 I.A.S. positions were held by women. In the Central Government, female employment was 3.6 percent of the

Table 4

Distribution of I.A.S. Officers at Selection Grade and Above by Sex in the States

Name and Scale	Total # of officers in position in the states	Men	Women	% Women to Total
1. Selection Grade (Rs. 2000-2250)	673	624	49	7.28
2. Super Time Scale				
i) (Rs. 2500-2700) Commissioner/Secretary in State or joint Secretary in Center	863	829	34	2.79
ii) (Rs. 3000-Fixed Member Board of Revenue/ Additional Secretary Government of India	173	161	12	6.93
iii) (Rs. 3500-Fixed Chief Secretary State Government/Secretary, Government of India	103	98	4	3.92
Total in Super-Time Scale	1,139	1,088	50	4.39

Source: Guha, 1975.

Table 5

Promotion of Women Officers to Selection Grade and Super Time Scale
1950-1982

Care of Officers	Total	Men	Women	% Women of Total
Initial in-take	3,062	2,769	281	9.17
Service of 14 yrs (1951-1964)	815	765	28	3.43
Service of 18 yrs (1951-1968)	1,303	1,217	64	4.90

Source: Guha et.al. 1984.

total in 1981. Of these, approximately 80 percent were concentrated in Class III clerical level jobs. The State Administrative Services are even worse. The state of Bihar in 1984 had no more than 30 to 35 women in a total of over 4000 Class II administrative service jobs. While the Constitution of India calls for equal treatment, the government does not have an Emancipation Committee or any other such mechanism to promote the entry of women into administration. The low educational and economic status of women combined with the traditional social norms which continue to support the wife/mother role model for Indian women mitigate against change. Marriage continues to be the main vocation for women. For a woman, taking a job suggests financial instability in the family, especially for those in the middle class. Males with working female family members are deemed unable to provide for their families. While these social norms have reluctantly condoned the entry of women into teaching, medicine, nursing and other "female" occupations, they are still unable to sanction women as administrators. This is the backdrop within which the present research on women administrators in India has occurred.

THE EMPIRICAL STUDY

The data presented in this paper compare administrators from the Union Territory of Delhi, a comparatively developed corner of the country with administrators from the Bihar state government, a region which is economically less developed in terms of urbanization and male to female literacy ratio. While the Delhi Union Territory is highly urbanized (93 percent), Bihar is one of the most backward states in India with only 12 percent of its population in urban areas (Lal 1981, Series 4). In Delhi, 53 percent of the females and 84 percent of the males are literate (Bhalla 1981, Series 28). In Bihar, only 14 percent of the females and 38 percent of the males are literate.

The methodology of the study involved identifying and interviewing women administrators using an appropriately modified version of the interview schedule and questionnaire developed by the international research group. (In each country, researchers had to modify the original research design slightly to make it applicable to the culture, language, and norms of the country being investigated.) The Delhi Administration (equivalent of the Delhi state) sample includes two categories, the I.A.S. and the "others," whereas the Bihar sample consists of three categories, the I.A.S., the State Services, and "others." The "others" category in Bihar consists of local officials such as municipal officers, block development officers, city corporation officers, and village panchayat officials. In Delhi, the "others" category includes these local officials as well as the State Services. In Delhi, the total number of officers was 1000 (excluding technical and medical college and hospital staff) of whom 20 percent were women. Fifty of the 1000 were I.A.S. officers, 10 of whom (20 percent) were women (Director 1983). In Bihar, female I.A.S. officers numbered less than 20 (6 percent) out of a total of 349. In the Provincial Civil Service (P.C.S.) of Bihar State Administrative Services, women numbered roughly 30 (0.8 percent) out of a total of 4000 (Department of Personnel and Administrative Reforms 1983).

The data. In each state, questionnaires were distributed to all female administrators in the designated top ranks mentioned above. Of the approximately 80 persons in the universe, 38 responded; 19 from Delhi and 19 from Bihar. The questionnaires, which were usually completed by the respondents in their homes, were followed with in-depth interviews which occurred in the respondents' offices. Tape recorders were not used. Each respondent was visited three to four times by the researcher to obtain the responses. In general, the response was better from administrators in Delhi. Also, women in the I.A.S. tended to be more cooperative than administrators in the State Services.

Socialization and education of family members. Only one of the respondents was born in a village. All of the other respondents were born in either a city or a town. The greater urbanization of Delhi was reflected in the fact that among the I.A.S., 60 percent of the Delhi women were born in the city, while 50 percent of the Bihar I.A.S. were born in the city. However, in the "others" category, all of the Delhi respondents were born in the city, and all of those from Bihar were born in towns. In both

I.A.S. and "other" categories, 83 percent of the Delhi women were born in cities, while only 24 percent of the Bihar women were born in cities.

With regard to family background for both states, 51 percent of the respondents belonged to nuclear families by birth, the remainder were members of joint or extended families. In Delhi, 56 percent of the I.A.S. belonged to nuclear families, whereas in Bihar, 100 percent of the I.A.S. women were from nuclear families. In the "others" category, 44 percent of the Delhi women were in nuclear families, while none of the Bihar "others" women belonged to nuclear families. In Bihar, 33 percent of the State Administrative Services women belonged to nuclear families.

In education, most respondents indicated that their parents had a high level of education. Only 3 percent of the respondents' fathers, and only 6 percent of the respondents' mothers were illiterate. Among the fathers, 34 percent were college graduates, and 26 percent had done post-graduate work. Among the mothers, 17 percent were college graduates, and 20 percent had done post-graduate work. About 22 percent of the sample did not respond. With regard to professions, most fathers (31 percent) were in government service, 17 percent were professionals (lawyers, doctors, engineers), and only 6 percent were farmers. Of the mothers, 8 percent were professionals, 9 percent were teachers, and 40 percent were housewives. None of the respondents had mothers who were administrators, while many of the fathers of the respondents were in the I.A.S. or the State Administrative Services.

Of the women administrators themselves, 74 percent were married and 26 percent were unmarried. Love marriages predominated with 54 percent of the respondents having such a marriage while 35 percent reported having an arranged marriage. The average age at marriage for all married respondents was 27 years old. The I.A.S. women had an average marriage age of 30 years; for the State Service women, the average marriage age was 27 years; and for "others," the average age was 19 years. For India as a whole, over 50 percent of the women marry between the ages of 15 and 19 years (Seager and Olsen 1986, 2). In this study, most of the respondents married late and are involved in a love marriage. This is an index of the modernity of the respondents as love marriages still are not very common in India, nor are they sanctioned by the society. The husbands are well educated (44 percent have college degrees, while 54 percent have post-graduate degrees) and hold good jobs. Taken together, the respondents belong to a very high income group. This could have a beneficial effect on their behavior as administrators. Freedom from financial worries could make them more independent and free them from the temptations of corruption.

The respondents had planned small families. The maximum number of children for the Delhi I.A.S. women was 2, and the average number was 1. For those women in the "others" category, the maximum number of children was 5 and the average number was 3. In the Bihar sample, the maximum number of children for the I.A.S. and the P.C.S. is 3 and the average is 1. Most of these women are in a relatively young group (23-30). Women in the "others" category in Bihar are older (many in the 40 year age group) and the maximum number of children is 5. For all of India, the national child to woman ratio in 1981 was 5.46 per woman in the age group 15-49. The State of Bihar had an average of 6 per woman which is above the national average (Raza and Nuna 1985, 16).

When asked about the children's education, 57 percent responded in favor of education through English medium schools. English medium, mission, and public schools have traditionally been the training grounds for bureaucratic and professional elites, and the majority of the most successful in India send their children to such schools. These schools are considered a passage to elite status in the country.

In religious persuasion, 71 percent of the total sample belonged to the Hindu community. Forty five percent belonged to the so called "upper castes." Sikhs are the next largest religious group with 16 percent of the total. The Christian religion claimed the allegiance of 11 percent of the respondents. Only one respondent was Muslim. Among the Hindu respondents, 45 percent were of the high caste, 13 percent were from backward castes, 3 percent were from the scheduled caste, and 11 percent were from Scheduled Tribes. The upper caste Hindu women clearly are the most highly represented group. The majority also belonged to the high income group — 44 percent from Delhi and 29 percent from Bihar.

Education. In educational attainment, the female administrators are a highly specialized group. A graduate degree is the minimum requirement for sitting in competitive examinations for administrative service, both Class I and Class II. The sample of women administrators had a higher number of post graduate degrees (66 percent) than graduate degrees (34 percent). Some of those with a B.A. degree also had a special degree in education or law. One had a diploma in Public Administration and Personnel. While 89 percent had degrees from Indian universities, 11 percent also had foreign degrees. One woman in the Bihar Education Service had a Ph.D. from the London School of Economics and Political Science, while two in the I.A.S. had degrees from Oxford and Cambridge. Of those in the total sample, 66 percent attended English medium schools, public, private, or mission, while only 29 percent attended Hindi medium schools. None of the I.A.S had attended Hindi medium schools, whereas none of the women in the State Services had attended English schools. The conclusion is that schooling in the English medium schools is important for success in Class I Competitive Examinations.

Career entry. The average age of joining the service for the respondents was 24 years of age. Over half of the sample (52 percent) had a job prior to joining the Administrative Services, usually college teaching. Of the I.A.S. in Delhi, 60 percent were between 31 and 35 years old. In Bihar, 38 percent of the I.A.S. women were 23 to 30 years old, 25 percent were 36-40 years old, and only 13 percent were in the 41-45 age group. None of the I.A.S. women in either the Delhi or Bihar samples was over 45. In the State Services in Bihar, 71 percent of the respondents were between 23 and 30. In the "other" category, two women were over 56 years old, and in the State Service, one woman was between 51 and 55. These age data suggest that entry into the I.A.S. and the State Services is a very recent trend for women.

When asked for their motivations in choosing an administrative career, 57 percent of the respondents mentioned the security of the job. The high status of the career was mentioned by 55 percent of the respondents. Good pay and power satisfaction were other factors that the respondents mentioned.

The very low numbers of women in the administrative services are due to a number of factors. The low literacy rate among Indian women combined with the high entry standards for Administrative Service requiring a graduate degree and success in competitive examinations mean that the pool of eligible women is very small. In addition, social norms discourage women from entering the Administrative Services. Administrative jobs are considered tough, unfeminine, and unsafe, as administrators must meet with the public and manage situations of violence during festivals and on other occasions. If a woman does manage to be a successful administrator, she is considered 'lacking' in feminine qualities.

The respondents themselves reflected this set of social norms as 39 percent of them expressed a preference for a medical career for their daughters. For 35 percent of the sample, the I.A.S. was the first choice for their daughters' careers. None of the respondents preferred that their daughters enter the Indian Police Services or the Foreign Service.

Discrimination. The majority of the I.A.S. respondents reported that they do not face problems within the administrative structure due to their sex. The rules are neutral and affect men and women in the same ways. A few states in India do discriminate with regard to giving "field postings" to women; however, neither the State of Bihar nor the Delhi Metropolitan area do this. The majority of the respondents have taken "field postings" such as Sub-Divisional Officer (S.D.O.) or District Magistrate which involve, among other duties, the maintenance of law and order in the area. They have even participated in patrolling duty during tense situations involving religious and caste riots. These women have held court and attended to semi-judicial duties. While an occasional case of sexual harassment occurs by a senior colleague or even a batch-mate (who entered the Service at the same time) (Committee to Examine Problems 1972), such behavior is exceptional rather than normal. The subordinate staff generally are "too much in 'awe' of the I.A.S. Officer to be offensive." Some Administrators reported that they had at times deliberately been posted to a department "to clear up the dirty mess created by a previous male officer." One of the I.A.S. Officers in Bihar is known as the "tough lady" and is often asked to handle a department which is in bad shape.

When asked about pressures from political bosses, the I.A.S. respondents reported that politicians are often reluctant to "get tough" with female I.A.S. Officers in the same way as they do with male I.A.S. Officers. The female officers displayed a certain degree of fearlessness in dealing with political pressures. However, the respondents from the State Service were not satisfied with their jobs. They felt that the senior male officers displayed some degree of hostility toward their female colleagues. Some felt that they were not taken "seriously." Postings in small places, especially suburban areas had problems of safety and lack of social life. Women posted as Block Development Officers had problems in conducting office work smoothly. The lower the degree of urbanization, the more the women reported problems of cordial interaction with male colleagues and subordinates. The feudal structure and norms maintain their sway the farther one is from metropolitan centers. Females belonging to the State Services and especially those in the early stages of their careers are considered quite insignificant. They have to face the arrogance of the local political leaders in their jurisdictions.

Promotions. While promotion is normally a routine matter for both males and females, 51 percent of the total sample agreed that they as women did not have equal access to higher positions in comparison to their male colleagues. In identifying the reasons, 53 percent of the respondents mentioned biology and 59 percent mentioned women's lack of ambition to reach the top. A large number of respondents (65 percent) mentioned family interference as the major reason for the lack of upward mobility among women. Women often had to sacrifice the chance to take tough and challenging jobs which sometimes promotion demanded because they had to have a 'posting' convenient to their husbands and children. Another group (24 percent) agreed that women lack the strength for the rigorous training necessary for handling tough jobs. In general in India, when a woman passes the Competitive Examinations and secures a post in administration, she is promoted at the same rate as her male colleagues. While female administrators are not denied promotion, they are denied appointments in more prestigious departments such as finance, or home or external affairs. Women are generally given positions in education, social welfare, or family-planning departments, while positions in more prestigious departments go to men. Rarely do women go to "tough" departments. In the Delhi Administration, one female is posted as deputy secretary Vigilance, which is a "tough" post for a female. Similarly in Bihar, one I.A.S. officer is the Managing Director of the State Financial Corporation. Some states in India do not give women district positions, because a District Magistrate frequently has to deal with law and order problems.

CONCLUSION

The data about female administrators in two regions of India, one forward looking and developed and the other backward, reveal a few general conclusions about the situation of women administrators in India. The barriers to women's advancement occur primarily at the educational and socialization levels in India. Once a woman enters a particular cadre of the administrative structure in India, either all India or State Services, she is legally treated as an equal with male colleagues. Promotions are generally based on length of service and service records for both men and women. Female I.A.S. Officers were very confident in reporting that they felt that no discrimination existed within the Indian Administrative Services. Women in the State Services expressed more reservations concerning this matter. Yet, reporting that no discrimination exists, the respondents note that while women are able to obtain the rank they are entitled to on the basis of seniority and service, they often fail to obtain the important posts such as Finance Commissioner, Secretary of Home Affairs, or Secretary of External Affairs. In some states, women have not held deputy district commissioner posts. Most often, women are placed in the Education and Culture or the Health Departments (Vithayathil 1971).

The working conditions for female administrators and the attitudes of male colleagues and the public at large often constitute barriers for women administrators. One female I.A.S. Officer openly complained that females in the I.A.S. are treated as second class citizens and that competent female officers are not given the opportunity to work in challenging jobs because of sex bias (Vitayathil 1971). Women are very aware of their minority status in the organization (Swarna Lata 1982 and Seethramu 1981). "As women come to accept by convention their minority roles, they gradually become a 'silenced group' as far as their organizations are concerned" (Amundsen 1971, 91). The State of Maharashtra established a committee to examine the problem facing female employees required to travel to the villages and stay there overnight. These women were having difficulty finding suitable accommodations. Furthermore, the orthodox rural population in the region believed that dealing with unmarried female employees was improper (Maharashtra Government Committee Report 1972, 36-37). The hostile attitude of the rural population toward women has also been noted by others. The eminent sociologist M.N. Srinivas stated in a 1976 lecture that "Traditionally, the Collector was regarded as the Lord of his district, and it is something of a cognitive revolution for villagers to find that they are being governed by a woman, and a young one at that" (Srinivas 1978).

In general, the female respondents in the Indian sample reaffirm the fact that the roles and behavior patterns expected of women have not changed much. In almost all societies, the most clearly defined role for women has been that of mother and wife. Motherhood as distinct from fatherhood has traditionally been viewed as a full-time job. Even when employed outside of the home, women tend to remain responsible for the mothering and general housekeeping functions (Davidson, Sirburg and Hill 1974, 185-188). For men, role differentiation within the family complements their occupational role achievement, whereas for women, this role differentiation frustrates outside role achievement (Stewart 1976, 357). For the success of the male, the wife role requires the woman to meet fully the stereotype definitions of the feminine supporter, comforter, childbearer, housekeeper, and entertainer (Papnek 1973, 852-872). These comments and conclusions made about men and women in Western societies are even more accurate in describing men and women in India. Indian women experience discrimination even more intensely because of the sex segregated character of the society, the conditions of poverty, and the traditional value system (Souza 1975, 13). As Mandelbaum notes, the typical Indian woman knows of no acceptable alternative role other than that of wife and mother (Mandelbaum 1974, 16). The wife-mother syndrome pervades the behavior and role performance of all women in India to some extent and socializes all women to avoid success, to be unambitious and to be passive even if they have gained admittance into the administrative service cadres (Lynn and Vaden 1978, 209).

The respondents in this study of India support the contention that family interference is the biggest obstacle to the career advancement of female administrators in India. This factor is closely followed by what appears to be the passivity and lack of ambition among women administrators. Most female administrators in India are married and they give higher priority to home and family life than they do to their own career advancement. Weighted with the duties and obligations imposed by cultural traditions and norms, many must do double duty to meet their professional demands. This phenomenon provides both an inner psychological and an explicitly overt set of constraints on women administrators.

Women in India are passing through the twilight zone of tradition and modernity. The growth of education, the extension of vocational and professional opportunities, and to some extent, the scarcity of financial resources for a large number of people are factors which are opening the gates of change for women. To say that women place a greater priority on home and family life than they do on professional life is *not* to say that women do not have ambition or that they do not desire power and independent decision-making authority. Caught between the home and the office, such women in India are engaged in a tough struggle for a viable position. Many of them have had to succumb to the pressures of family and home and try to be content with a mediocre service record. Whether this will continue to be the pattern in the future is not clear.

REFERENCES

Amundsen, Kirsten. 1971. *The Silenced Majority: Women and American Democracy*. Engelwood Cliffs, N.J.: Prentice-Hall.

Bhalla, V.K. 1982. *Census of India 1981*. Paper 1 of 1982. Series 28. Delhi: Director of Census Operation.

Committee to Examine the Problems Facing Women Employees in Government Services. 1972. *Report*. Bombay: Government of Maharashtra.

Davidson, K.M., R.B. Sirburg, and H.K. Hill. 1974. "Marriage and Family Life" in *Sex-Based Discrimination: Text, Cases and Materials*. St. Paul, Minn: West Publishing Co.

Department of Personnel and Administrative Reforms. 1983. Patna: Government of Bihar.

Department of Personnel and Administrative Reforms, Ministry of Home Affairs. 1984. "Civil List of the Indian Administrative Service as on 1.1.84" ed. 29. New Delhi: Controller of Publications, Government of India.

Director, Delhi Metropolitan Administration. 1983. Personal Communication. Delhi.

Guha, P. et al. Committee on the Status of Women in India. 1975. "Towards Equality." New Delhi: Department of Social Welfare, Ministry of Education and Social Welfare, Government of India.

Lal, B.B. 1981. *Census of India 1981 Supplement*. Paper 1 of 1982. Series 4. Delhi: Director of Census Operations.

Lynn, N., and R.E. Vaden. 1978. "Towards a Non-Sexist Personnel Opportunity Structure—The Federal Executive Bureaucracy" in *Public Administrator*.

Maharashtra Government Committee Report. 1972. Bombay: Government of Maharashtra.

Mandelbaum, D.J. 1974. *Human Fertility in India*. Berkeley and Los Angeles: University of California Press.

Mitra, A. et al., eds. 1980. *The Status of Women: Shifts in Occupational Participation 1961-1971*. New Delhi: Abhinav Publications.

Padmanabh, P. 1983. "Primary Census Abstract: General Population," *Census of India 1981*. Series 1. India. Part II B (i), (iii). New Delhi: Registrar General and Census Commissioner, India.

Papnek, Hanna. January, 1973. "Men, Women and Work: Reflections on the Two-Person Career." *American Journal of Sociology* 78: 852-872.

Raza Moonis, and S.C. Nuna. 1985. "Map of India-Births: Four and Above" and "Child/Woman Ratio 1981." *Population and Development: Towards the 21st Century*. New Delhi: The Family Planning Foundation.

Reserve Bank of India. October, 1978. "Reserve Bank of India Bulletin." Bombay: Reserve Bank of India.

Seager, Joni, and Ann Olson. 1986. *Women in the World: An International Atlas*. NY: Simon & Schuster.

Seethramu, A.S. 1981. *Women in Organized Movements*. New Delhi: Ambika Publications.

Souza, De A., ed. 1975. *Women in Contemporary India: Traditional Images and Changing Roles*. New Delhi: Manahar Publications.

Srinivas, M.N. 1978. *The Changing Position of Indian Women*. Delhi: Oxford University Press.

Stewart, Debra. July-August, 1976. "Women in Top Jobs." *Public Administration Review* 36 (4).

Swarna Lata. October-December, 1982. "Women in All India Services." *Prashashnika*. vol.2 (4). Jaipur: The A.C.M. Institute of Public Administration.

Vitayathil. 1971. "Women in the I.A.S." *Journal of National Academy of Administration*. Mussoori: National Academy of Administration.

Women in State Administration in the People's Republic of Bulgaria

Nora Ananieva
Evka Razvigorova

HISTORICAL BACKGROUND

Historically, Bulgarian women have been politically active in the anti-fascist and national liberation struggle of the Bulgarian people. Bulgarian women fought heroically during the April uprising of 1876 against Ottoman bondage; they took to arms and fought shoulder to shoulder with men in the first anti-fascist uprising in the world in September, 1923. Tens of thousands of women took part in the anti-fascist struggle and contributed to the socialist revolution of September, 1944.

The Bulgarian Communist Party is a more recent force which has consistently supported political rights for women. As early as 1891, at its Constituent Assembly, the party of Bulgarian Social Democrats proclaimed as a top political priority the achievement of social and political equality for women and took efficient measures to that effect. For the founding father of the Bulgarian Social Democratic party, Dimiter Blagoev, "The problem of women's emancipation coincides with the problem of the economic emancipation of mankind" (Dimitrov 1979). For nearly a hundred years, the Communist Party's policy line on the issue of women's emancipation was an integral part of its general political and socio-economic strategy.

One of the first normative deeds passed by the People's government in 1944 was the law granting equal juridical rights to persons of both sexes. The equality of men and women became a constitutional principle in the Constitution of 1947. Article 36 of the present constitution states: "Men and Women in the People's Republic of Bulgaria enjoy equal rights." The principle of equality was further specified in many other provisions of the constitution. For example, Article 35, paragraph 3, obligates the state to

31

secure equality by creating the conditions and providing the opportunities for the equal exercise of all rights and obligations. The same principle underlies the overall constitutional development of the system of rights, liberties, and obligations of the citizens of the People's Republic of Bulgaria as well as the whole legislative system. In this sense, the problem of Bulgarian women's political rights and liberties has been solved both constitutionally and legislatively.

The progressive thinkers from the time of the bourgeois revolutions did not identify equality of rights with actual equality. They stressed the relationship between juridical, political, and social reality. They believed that the problem of women's active participation in political life could not be reduced to the equality of rights or to the constitutional treatment of political rights and liberties. Women's participation involved a whole complex of material, social, political, and legislative preconditions for the complete and exact reflection of the will and interests of women. The presence of women in politics had not only direct, but also indirect consequences which reflect the general dynamics of socio-economic development and the maturity of social relations.

In the first years of Soviet rule, Lenin wrote: "We really razed to the ground the infamous laws placing women in a position of inequality . . . But the more we have cleared the ground of the lumber of the old, bourgeois laws and institutions, the clearer it is to us that we have only cleared the ground to build on but are not yet building" (Lenin 1977, v. 29, 429). For Lenin, the return of women to the sphere of public production was the first prerequisite for social emancipation for women and for the achievement of real equality with men (Lenin 1977, v. 30, 43).

The major force motivating women to join the paid labor force in the wake of the socialist revolution in Bulgaria was the government's accelerated drive for socio-economic development and its general striving to overcome economic backwardness. The needs of the Bulgarian family also encouraged women's participation in the paid labor force. A third factor was women's desire for self-fulfillment, especially for the educated, politically oriented young women.

BULGARIAN WOMEN
IN THE LABOR FORCE

Bulgarian women have always been working women. The census of 1946 showed that women constituted 45 percent of the economically active population (Dinkova 1980, 16). But in the then backward agrarian society, women usually worked as farm and other laborers. The present picture of women's employment in the People's Republic of Bulgaria shows three important trends which are relevant to the advent of women in state administration.

First, many women have moved into new professions and into new technological industries. In 1946, women constituted 7.8 percent of all manual workers, 1.4 percent of employees, and 1.3 percent of university and vocational college graduates. In 1984, the percentage of women engaged in industry, in various services, and in government jobs rose to 49.3 percent of the total labor force. At present, every third engineer in Bulgaria is a woman. Women have also been flowing steadily into the non-production spheres of the economy. In 1984, the relative share of women in health services, education, the arts, and culture rose to 66 percent. One half of the country's physicians are women while over 70 percent of the teaching and research staffs at all levels of education are also women. Women have also been moving into the governmental sphere where they hold not only ancillary but also decision-making positions. Women compose 29.8 percent of the entire managerial cadre, 45 percent of the total number of judges, and 30 percent of all lawyers in Bulgaria. Women have also been taking professional jobs in agriculture. In 1984, the number of female agricultural specialists was four times as high as it was in 1960: 41.7 percent of all agronomists and 36% of all livestock experts were women (Women in the People's Republic of Bulgaria 1984.)

A second important trend involves changes in women's motivation to work. A representative sociological study conducted in 1980 entitled "Women in the Economic, Public, Cultural and Family Life" included the question: "If your family and you enjoyed economic security, would you continue to work?" Only 15.8 percent of all women answered in the affirmative. Asked the same question five years later, that percentage fell (Women and Labour 1980, 58-78). In spite of these statistics, for many contemporary Bulgarian women, especially for the young and the middle aged, work has become a spiritual need, a most important factor for self-fulfillment.

A third trend is the increasing involvement of women in the management and organization of production. By 1984, a total of 56,485 persons were engaged in top levels of management and administration. Of these, 53.8 percent were women.

Critical to this involvement in the labor force are the strides which women have made in becoming educated. Here, women have achieved almost complete equality. In 1946, women with higher education were only 0.4 percent of the economically active population. Before the socialist revolution, many institutes of higher education, including the law schools, excluded women. By 1985, 47.6 percent of all those in the labor force with higher education were women; and 52.3 percent of all university graduates were women. Finally, the desire for self-fulfillment gave women a particular incentive to obtain higher education. The number of women in vocational training is also rising quickly.

A number of decisions by the Party and the Government facilitated the movement of women into management positions, especially policies which aided women in their other functions related to childcare and home-making. Not surprisingly, women in Bulgaria are politically most active at their working places. About 47.6 percent of the trade union elective bodies are composed of women, and women are also quite active in the local bodies. Women have also been moving into elective offices. In the National Assembly, 21.8 percent of the membership are women and 33.6 percent of the members of the local elected bodies are women. Compared to the Parliament of 1945 where 5 percent of the members were women, these percentages signal an enormous improvement. However, when half of the labor force consists of women, when over half of the university graduates and activists in the local trade unions and other public organizations are also women, these percentages have been rising at an extremely slow pace over the past 10 years.

WOMEN IN STATE ADMINISTRATION: A STUDY

State administration in Bulgaria in 1985 had a double meaning: in a narrow sense, it meant the total number of executive bodies; in a broader sense, it included all the institutions, including the Board of the National Assembly (the supreme representative body of state power), the State Council, the Council of Ministers, the people's councils (the territorial bodies of power including the district, municipal councils and city councils), and the lawcourts. The state administration also included the bodies of the Council of Ministers for economic management and management of the non-production sphere (ministries and committees).

Within state administration were two types of positions: appointive posts (associates, advisors, directors, deputy ministers and heads of departments) and elective posts (chairmen, deputy chairmen of the people's councils, members of the State Council, chairmen and deputy chairmen of the district people's councils and the municipal councils and mayors). The appointive posts were occupied by people chosen for their performance as they have ascended the hierarchical ladder. The elective posts were held by politically active persons who also should have managerial experience. For this study, twenty women of both categories at all levels of state administration were included. The posts held by the sample of twenty women included: deputy chairman, National Assembly (elected); advisor, Council of Ministers (appointed); member of the State Council (elected); advisor to State Council (appointed); four deputy chairmen of Regional People's Council (elected); four deputy chairmen of Municipal Councils (elected); two deputy ministers and one director of a Ministry (appointed); and one elected and four appointed public prosecutors in the Law Courts.

The research methodology involved using questionnaires and interviews to solicit information from these twenty women occupying positions in the top levels of the state administrative hierarchy. Sociologist Branimir Botev conducted the interviews either in the workplace or in the homes of the interviewees.

Basic Description of the Data

As Table 1 indicates, 13 of the 20 women in the sample were over 50 years of age with all but one having had higher education. Interestingly, all but one had been married at one time and 17 were currently married at the time of the interview and the same number had children. Only one woman in the sample had a parent with an education higher than the secondary level.

Career History, Education, and Training

Each woman in the sample exhibited one of three different patterns of career development: Half of the women in the sample began work as a rank and file specialist in the area for which they had been professionally trained. This most often meant the performance of production tasks requiring the competence of university graduate specialists. The initial push from their specialties (usually the economic and the production sphere) was decisive for the further development of their careers.

The second career pattern was exhibited by women who started their careers as office workers, as administrative and organizational functionaries. Typically, this group of women started their social and political work during their school years and/or during the years of their higher education. These women found themselves performing social and political work without having an opportunity to use their educational specialties. Some of these women were educated as economists or as engineers. Most started their careers in regional management positions. A third career type that was not well represented in the sample defined those women who had

Table 1. Description of the Data

Age	Number
30-39	3
40-49	4
50-55	8
55+	5
Total	20

Type of Post	Number
elective office	11
appointment	9
Total	20

Education	Number
higher	19
college	1
Total	20

Family Status	Number
married	17
divorced/widowed	2
unmarried	1
Total	20

Children	Number
one	8
two	8
three	1
none	3
Total	20

Social Origin	Number
workers	8
peasants	4
employees	1
intelligentsia	1
no data	6
Total	20

Education of Both Parents	Number	Education of One Parent Only
no education	1	1 (mother)
elementary	-	3
primary	7	1 (mother)
secondary	3	1 (father)
higher	1	2

begun their careers as functionaries at the local level. The development of their careers generally remained in the same sphere of the economy and progressed from low to high level management. They obtained their educations while on the job. Only after reaching the highest levels of the local hierarchies did they move to administrative and organizational work in the regional organizations, the central state administration and/or political organizations.

Education

All of the people in this investigation were university graduates and over three fourths of them had obtained their diplomas prior to starting their careers in state administration (even at the lower level). A university degree appears to have been almost a prerequisite for employment in a management position in state administration. The remaining one fourth of the sample were most frequently described by the second or third type of career mentioned above. About 40 percent of the women were educated as economists; however, most of this group began their careers in administrative and organizational work and not in the economic sphere. The second largest group were educated as engineers, mostly chemical engineers and technologists. A few of these women began their careers in administrative positions outside of the production sphere. The education of the remainder of the sample was varied representing fields like law, pedagogy, social and political sciences, and agricultural sciences.

Motives for Career Choice:
Job Satisfaction and Self Assessment

Social prestige often determines the choice of the type of education a woman chooses, but the type of education often has little to do with the content of the job taken after graduation. Nearly half (45 percent) of the women in the sample stated that they were placed in administrative positions against their will and that they would prefer to be specialists in their professions rather than administrators. Typical were such statements as: "I have always wanted to be a specialist, not a functionary," "the decision for the transfer to the new post, to a responsible organizational position, was not my decision," "I am a teacher by profession and I have never wanted to be an administrator," "My love was for the children and the work as a teacher for 17 years and I came to this job almost with tears in my eyes. But work in the administrative and managerial field is a question of political decision and a personnel policy."

One reason for the dissatisfaction that women express with their managerial careers is related to the preliminary training and social expectations of women in Bulgarian society. About 30 percent of the women sampled specifically expressed a desire to perform administrative and managerial work. However, when questioned, they indicated that they were more motivated by the desire to work with people than by the desire to exercise power or by the opportunity for independent decision-making. Specific differences exist between men and women in this regard. Men connect their professional and personal self-satisfaction to a considerably greater degree with the status characteristics of the post they occupy and with the possibility for greater power. Women's motivations for the acceptance of a job in state administration are primarily connected with the possibility of working with people.

The remaining 25 percent of the sample did not express any particular attitude towards the development of their careers. They considered their careers part of a natural process whereby, during the course of their working life, their strengths had been assessed and properly directed. Only one woman had a family tradition of management careers. She had parents who were directly involved in state management and she herself had started to do social and organizational work as a teenager. In summary, the career development of women in administration depends more on the initial talents of women as specialists and on the needs of the organization rather than on the personal desires and goals of the women themselves.

Self Assessment

One segment of the interview asked the respondents to assess their own social recognition and prestige in the eyes of other people. About 40 percent of the women (mainly those who preferred their specialty to their administrative jobs) thought that the main recognition they have received had come from their specialist colleagues and not from the status of the administrative position they now hold. All of the women interviewed considered their prestige to be high enough in the eyes of the organization in which they hold an administrative post; however, only a third of the women felt that the prestige they now command was due to the administrative post they now hold.

Prospects for career advancement is another indicator of the self assessment of women. Over 60 percent of the respondents sincerely state that they do not desire further promotion as administrators. Those who do have higher ambitions connect that ambition with the quality of the work to be performed, with the possibility for greater creativity, and with the improvement of their own qualifications. A second group of women desire promotion within the organization in which they now work, not for themselves but for the sake of the organization and its mission.

The Choice of Career
and Family-Career Relationships

The sample exhibited considerable divergence concerning the factors influencing their choice of career. One third of the women indicated that they made an independent choice. About 20 percent were influenced by their fathers. The remaining women were influenced by a variety of diverse factors: their relatives, the family as a whole, teachers, friends. The help and support which these women now have in their careers comes primarily from a narrow circle of colleagues and relatives. About 45 percent of the women mentioned their husbands. Most women felt that they had support and understanding from their husbands. In most cases, the qualifications of the husband and wife were about equal. In the sample of 18 married women, only two women had husbands who had less education than they. One husband had a secondary education and one had a college education. The remaining husbands all had higher education. One woman in the sample was divorced. One was a widow, and one was not married. One woman had three children; however, the rest had either one or two children. All the married women indicated that their husbands support them in principle, but that they still cannot always rely on their help in the family and household chores.

Half of the women interviewed specifically stated that no one helps them with the housekeeping work. One third indicated that their husbands help (an average of 10 hours per week), and the remainder of the women did not respond to this question. The majority (60 percent) of the sample stated that they would direct their own daughters towards a professional career. About 28 percent (5 women) stated a preference for the woman to pay more attention to the family, to be a good mother, wife, and housewife. Two women (11 percent) thought the best policy was to combine profession and family duties in an optimal way.

CONCLUSION

This study shows that women's careers in public administration are the result of a complex interaction of factors: economic, political, ideological, legal and socio-psychological. The socialist revolution gives priority to the political and ideological factors. The impact of these political and ideological changes, combined with the objective needs of accelerated social and economic development, have had a cumulative effect allowing women to enter all fields of public production in Bulgaria. The growing levels of education and training for women, which are the result of this process, in turn determines the inevitable march of women (although at a slower rate) into leading managerial positions in public administration. Critical to this process have been specific legal policies adopted by the state which have enhanced the ability of women to move into managerial positions. The unsolved problems that continue to present barriers to the advancement of women are due in part to the failure to adhere to these legal principles, in part to the practical difficulties of releasing women from their traditional daily chores, and in part to the subjective attitudes of both men and women regarding new roles for women.

REFERENCES

Dimitrov, Blagoev D.G. 1979. About Women and the Family. Sofia: Ot. Front.
Dinkova, M. 1980. The Social Portrait of the Bulgarian Woman. Sofia: Profizdat.
Lenin, *V.I. 1977.* Collected Works. Moscow: Progress.
Marx, K. and F. Engels. 1973. Sofia: BKP.
Women and Labour: On some Socio-economic Problems of the Employment of Working Women. 1980. Sofia: Profizdat.
Women in the People's Republic of Bulgaria: A Statistical Handbook. 1984. Sofia: Sofia Press.

Women in Public Administration in the Netherlands

Monique Leyenaar

This article reviews the current position of women in governmental service as well as the concrete policies taken by the government to increase the number of women employees. The first section describes the general situation of women in the labor market in the Netherlands with special attention to those in governmental service. The second section discusses the policies taken by the government to strengthen the position of its women employees. The last section contains the result of interviews held with women in the Department of Economics and discusses other research findings concerning barriers for the advancement of women in public administration.

WOMEN IN THE LABOR FORCE

In the Netherlands, unlike other countries of the European Community (EC), women have never been a large part of the labor force. From 1900 to 1960, women formed around one-fifth of the working population, a number which varied only slightly during this period. Significant changes did occur, however, in the kind of women who participated in wage labor. At the beginning of the century, 22.5 percent of the work force engaged in work outside of the home were women. Most were working class women and wives of shop-owners and farmers. A steady rise in the standard of living beginning in the fifties, a high postwar marriage rate, and the dictums of the Roman Catholic and Protestant churches that married women belong at home, caused the withdrawal of many married women from the labor market and generated a decline in the percentage of women in the working population from 24.4 percent in 1947 to 22.3 percent in 1960 (Central Bureau voor de Statistiek 1979, 1982). After 1960, the percentage of women in the paid labor force increased rapidly. During this period, married women from all social classes were largely responsible for this increase. Between 1960 and 1981, the proportion of employed married women rose from 7 percent to 33 percent. In 1960, women quit their jobs at the time of marriage; in 1979, they left when the first child was expected. Seventy-five percent of married women under 35 years of age without children were employed compared to 16 percent of the same group with small children (Oudijk 1984, 192).

Despite this rapid increase, the Netherlands have the lowest participation rate of women in wage labor in the European Community: 35 percent compared to an average of more than 50 percent (except for Ireland) in the other European Community countries. Some explanations are:

- the late start (end of the 19th century) of industrialization compared with Britain, France, and Belgium. At that time, capital had many cheap male workers at its disposal and no (great) need for women and children.
- the fact that the Netherlands were not involved either in the war of 1870 in Europe, nor in World War I. As a consequence, no shortage of men occurred.
- compared with other countries, the relatively high wages and social security benefits in the Netherlands permitted women to stay at home while their husbands were employed.
- the role of the Dutch churches, which propagated the ideology of family and motherhood.

The discrepancy in female labor market participation between the Netherlands and the other European Community countries is generated primarily by women over 25 years of age.

The increase in the number of working women does not mean, however, that the existing job segregation between women and men has disappeared. The expansion of the service and public sectors of the economy, both of which employ a large number of women, is responsible for this change. Of the employed women in 1981, 84 percent had jobs in the service and public sectors compared to 55 percent of the employed men. In 1963, 70 percent of the women and 41 percent of the men had jobs in these two sectors (Central Bureau voor de Statistiek 1979, 1982). This sex segregation of occupations has not changed in the 1970s and 1980s. One-third of all employed women work in four types of occupations: salespersons; secretaries or receptionists; administrative positions; and in 'caring' jobs such as nursing. (In comparison, one-third of all employed males work in 14 occupations.) The female labor force also differs in that half of the employed women work part-time, compared to only 5 percent of employed men, and in that women constitute only 7 percent of those in managerial and executive occupations (Oudijk 1984, 199).

Overall, the position of Dutch women in the labor market is one in which family responsibilities still determine the number of women in the paid labor force, as well as the kind and the level of the jobs women occupy. The organization of daily life takes the family with an employed husband and a wife at home as the norm.

WOMEN IN THE BUREAUCRACY

A critical examination of women employed in public administration is important for several reasons. First, in the Netherlands the government is the largest employer. Second, in 1981 almost half (49 percent) of all employed women were in the public sector, and third, activities performed by the public sector to improve the position of its women employees may serve as an example to other sectors.

The situation of women in public administration differs little from the general situation in the private sector. The overall percentage of women employed in governmental service in 1988 shows an increase compared with 1976 (Table 1).

Between 1976 and 1988, the number of women increased by more than 50 percent, but the relative growth was about 6 percent. That women administrators are still a long way from the top is illustrated by the huge income differences between women and men.

The Dutch Government uses six salary levels related to certain functions within the administration. Level I is the lowest and level VI is the highest. In 1985, of all women governmental employees, 82.9 percent

Table 1: Number of women in governmental service

Year	# of women (rounded)	% women of the total
1976	25,000	18.5
1979	27,500	19.1
1982	34,000	21.8
1984	34,000	22.7
1985	36,000	23.2
1988	41,000	24.6

Sources: Oudijk, 1984. and Ministerie van Binnenlandse Zaken 1985, 1986, 1989.

earned an income falling into the two lowest categories compared to 52.4 percent of all men. As Table 2 shows, by 1988 these figures had changed slightly with men still retaining an advantage over women in the overall distribution of income but also a slight advantage in the rate of increase in the top two salary levels. That women on the average are paid less than men can be explained only partly by the fact that women are on the average younger in age. Within each age category, women also are paid less than their male colleagues. Finally, more than one-third of the women in public service work part-time compared to only 2.5 percent of the men (Ministerie van Binnenlandse Zaken 1985, 5).

Besides the vertical segregation described above, horizontal segregation also exists. The percentage of women differs widely according to department.

At the time of the interviews in 1985, the percentages of women employed in the Department of Transport and the Department of Education varied from 14.2 percent to 37.5 percent respectively. Eight departments employed more than 30 percent women administrators and five had less than the average of 23.2 percent. Among the latter are the Departments of Finance, Agriculture, Transport, and Defense, all sectors where women have not been employed traditionally. Table 3 indicates that between 1985 and 1988, all departments except Justice increased the percentage of women slightly.

Summarizing, the increase in the percentage of women employed in public administration is small; in most years not even 1 percent per year.

Table 2: Income position of women and men in public administration 1985 and 1988

Salary level	Women(%)		Men(%)		Total	
	1985	1988	1985	1988	1985	1988
I (scale 1-3)	35.3	25.2	17.8	12.2	21.9	15.4
II (scale 4-6)	47.6	48.9	34.5	27.6	37.6	32.8
III (scale 7-9)	11.5	17.2	29.5	38.7	25.3	33.4
IV (scale 10-12)	5.2	7.2	14.8	16.2	12.6	14.0
V (scale 13-15)	0.5	1.2	2.5	4.0	2.0	3.3
VI (scale 16)	0.1	0.3	0.8	1.3	0.6	1.1
Total %	100	100	100	100	100	100
Total Number	36,380	41,069	120,400	127,767	156,786	166,836

Source: Ministry of Internal Affairs, 1985, 1989.

Table 3: Percentage of Women the Different Departments. 1985. 1988

Department	1985	1988	Total in Department 1985
Education	37.5	39.0	4,269
General Affairs	36.1	39.2	441
Internal Affairs	34.9	34.6	3,419
Culture	34.8	34.8	8,034
Justice	34.0	25.7	19,119
Foreign Affairs	31.8	39.0	1,748
Employment and Social Security	31.7	34.6	7,395
Economic Affairs	27.3	28.4	6,761
Housing and Environment	22.5	23.9	8,591
Agriculture and Fisheries	22.1	22.2	11,201
Finance	19.8	23.7	34,458
Defense	16.0	17.8	29,534
Transport	14.2	16.5	20,367

Source: Ministerie van Binnenlandse Zaken. 1985, 1989.

Furthermore, within the departments, women employees experienced very little upward mobility.

A CASE STUDY:
THE DEPARTMENT OF ECONOMICS

To obtain more information concerning the structural and psychological barriers that exclude women from the higher echelons of the public service, all twelve women employees in scales IV, V and VI (see Table 2) working at the Ministry of Economic Affairs were interviewed personally in the summer of 1985. At this time, 27.3 percent of the Department of Economic Affairs employees were female. The Department ranked eighth in the list of ministries with regard to the percentage of women employees (see Table 3). Since only 15 percent of all university economics students are female, the subject area of this department is regarded as a non-typical women's area. Those women in positions requiring a university degree in the department generally had a law degree. Table 4 shows that the earn-

Table 4: Income position of women and men working at the Department of Economics in 1985

Salary Level	Women %	Men %	Women & Men Total Number
I	34.0	10.2	
II	50.1	24.0	
III	9.7	30.0	
IV	5.6	29.3	
V	0.2	4.6	
VI	0.2	2.0	
Total %	100.0	100.0	
% of both Women and Men	27.3	72.7	

6761

Source: Ministry of Internal Affairs. 1985.

ings of 93 percent of the female employees in the Department fall in the lowest three categories compared to 74 percent of all the male employees.

Findings: personal background. The age of these twelve female civil servants varied between 32 and 64, with 75 percent of the interviewed women being between 32 and 40 years old. All held university degrees. Of these, seven were law degrees. Only one woman had a degree in economics. Of the interviewed women, two were married with very young children and four others lived with a partner. One woman had two children, two and four years old, the other had one child, two years old. The majority of those interviewed were still in doubt about starting a family. All recognized that motherhood would drastically diminish their career chances. They were aware of the negative attitudes of chiefs confronted with pregnancy and motherhood. The two mothers in the sample both worked full-time. One had a full-time childminder at home; the other had a husband who cared for the child. The department provided child care for only five children in a nearby center, and has made no other arrangements to accommodate the reproductive needs of its employees.

Findings: career planning. In the Netherlands, the public sector is organized in a strictly hierarchical way. Women in lower paying administrative positions have difficulty advancing into higher paying policy making or lower management jobs. For jobs that fall into salary level IV and upwards, a university degree is required. Entry begins in a junior policy making position and career advancement means a management job. The number of people one directs is indicative of the status of the job. At the time of this study only three women had a management position in the

Department of Economic Affairs. Most of the women who were interviewed expressed the wish to improve their career status. Surprisingly, almost none mentioned the desire to apply for a job in the private sector. The few who did not want to rise on the career ladder commented on the number of hours one is expected to work in management positions and the necessity of exposing oneself to tough competition.

Without exception, the interviewed women complained about the "lack of career guidance" from the personnel department. Although it is not a formal rule, in general, vacant higher management positions are not openly announced. Persons in question are usually asked to apply for the vacant job. Visibility consequently is very important. This leads to another complaint: the existence of an old boy's network. Male senior civil servants see each other frequently and divide the jobs between their own protégés. For example, the secretary-general of the Department of Economic Affairs has surrounded himself with young male newcomers mainly from the faculty of Economics of the University of Rotterdam (the university where the secretary-general himself is appointed for one day a week as a professor in economics). Practices of this kind lessen the chances for women to advance. A few women, however, mentioned that being one of the few women enhances one's visibility, which can be an advantage.

Findings: attitude towards women. The general attitude of department management towards the employment of women was positive. Many respondents noted that this depended largely on the attitude of top management. Some interviewed women stated that in contrast to most of the top managers, middle management is more conservative in its attitude. Many middle managers still consider the hiring of women as a risk, since women as a group may need special arrangements such as flexible working hours, maternity leave, and sick leave to care for their children. For such middle managers, two women on their staff of ten is more than enough.

Within the Department of Economics in 1983, a working group was established, called "het Emancipatieberaad" (the Emancipation Council), to advise the personnel department on internal policy making concerning the employment and advancement of women. This group organizes regular meetings for women employees in the department. One of the results of the working group was that after a survey organized to assess the need for child care, a facility for five children was created.

Findings: gender differences in work styles. The view that women administrators function differently from men is held by quite a few researchers of management styles and was again confirmed by the interviewed women. The perceived differences did not concern the content or the outcome of their work, but were more related to how the work was done. A large majority (10 of the 12 interviewees) identified the following differences:

- a less hierarchical attitude and behavior towards the secretarial staff.
- an intention to discuss problematic matters bilaterally first, before bringing them to the attention of higher placed administrators (less competitive).
- an eye for personal problems of the staff and an openness to discuss these problems (other directed caring).
- a need to socialize with colleagues (mingling of private and working matters).

Findings: positive discrimination. Although formally positive action is part of governmental policies, most of the interviewed women administrators are strongly opposed to the use of a quota. Only three women took a positive stand, stressing the fact that the position of women in the public service needed this catching-up maneuver. For them, an even better policy would be the replacement of one-third of the higher management by women at one time. The women opposed to quota setting noted the dangers of stigmatization. When employees were not appointed on the basis of their capacities, but because of their sex, a devaluation of all women in higher positions can be one of the consequences. In addition, it appeared from the interviews that many respondents are not attracted to feminism and feminists. Although a majority were in favor of equal opportunity policies, these women associated feminism with demonstrating and rioting.

On the whole, the interviewed women were not very satisfied with the career opportunities within the Department. Although they perceived the attitude of the Department towards women employees as fairly positive, they believed much still needed to be done about career guidance. In their view, the main problem was the lack of structural adaptations within the organization, making it easier for women to combine working outside the house with rearing children. Many people within the bureaucracy still hold the view that despite the differences in roles, no exceptional measures should be taken for women. To put it bluntly, a woman administrator sees her career ending the moment she decides to become a mother. Although the general attitude of the Department towards hiring women is positive, the Department refuses to create the more flexible organization that women need in matters of working hours, child care facilities, and career opportunities.

Findings from other studies. These conclusions are supported by other studies probing similar issues. In a survey among women working in local government, an open-ended question asked whether the women experienced barriers (and if so, which) in their task performance. One-third of the interviewed women mentioned the lack of career prospects, inflexible working hours, and the unaccommodating arrangements for leave as barriers, while 18 percent identified problems related to the organizational structure such as the hierarchical decision structure and the male dominated work-culture (Kring van Gemeentersecretarissen 1985, 42).

Table 5 illustrates the remarkably large difference between women and men in their wish for career advancement, and the fact that pregnancy is by far the most important reason women give for quitting their jobs in the civil service. The study indicates further that 31 percent of the women who resigned for reasons of pregnancy would have considered continuing to work if a day nursery had been available; 20 percent of them would have remained if a part-time job had been offered to them; and 49 percent would have left anyhow. Both men and women were asked what sort of circumstances at work constituted a reason to leave. The important reasons for men were: the low salary level available to them, the lack of career prospects, and the work atmosphere. Women employees, however, stressed the work atmosphere and the monotony of their work, but the salary level meant much less to them (Ministerie van Binnenlandse Zaken 1984, 11).

Table 5: Reasons for resignation

	Women%*	Men%*
Promotion opportunities elsewhere	16	72
Circumstances at work	18	38
Pregnancy	50	--
Personal circumstances	28	18

Total number of responses for both men and women was 308.

* more than one response was allowed

Source: Ministerie van Binnenlandse Zaken. 1985.

EQUAL OPPORTUNITY POLICIES

Against the background of the "second emancipation wave" of the late sixties, the government began in 1974 to adopt policies to improve the position of women in the labor market. The Ministry of Culture, Recreation, and Social Work (CRM) which was in charge of the coordination of emancipation policy at that time, established two governmental committees: a National Committee "Year of the Women," and an Advisory Committee for Emancipation. Amid some controversy, the latter managed to produce about one hundred recommendations. The government had not solicited most of this advice and chose to ignore most of it. The following recommendations from the Committee, however, were transformed into actual policy.

- the appointment in 1977 of an under-secretary for emancipation, attached to the Department of Culture, Recreation and Social Work. (The first under-secretary was a Christian-Democrat. She was succeeded in 1981 by a member of the Dutch Labor Party. The last under-secretary was from the Liberal Party. By 1985, the Minister of Social Affairs and Employment had assumed responsibility for this policy area.)

- the designation of emancipation as "facet policy," meaning that women's liberation was not a phenomenon to be isolated in one department; it should instead be an aspect of policy in every department. In 1977, the government established an interdepartmental committee for emancipation policy (ICE). Members of intradepartmental committees represented their departments in the ICE.

- the establishment of a Council for Emancipation to succeed the Advisory Committee for Emancipation. One consequence of the "facet policy" of emancipation was that Ministers from other departments were *obliged* to ask the Council's advice on every piece of legislation they planned to introduce.

During the first period, roughly from 1974 to 1981, the goal of governmental emancipation policy was to change people's attitudes, opinions and mentalities concerning the roles of women and men. Education was considered the proper weapon to attack current beliefs with regard to men and women and to prevent future prejudice. Second Chance Comprehensive schools for "mothers" attracted a large number of eager students. Meanwhile, sons and daughters were educated using properly screened teaching material, in which papa did not merely "fume une pipe" but washed the dishes as well. As time progressed, more and more people came to realize that the inferior position of women in society was fundamentally rooted in social-economic structures. As a consequence, the under-secretary and her administrative staff were moved from the Department of Culture, Recreation, and Social Work (CRM) to the Ministry of Employment and Social Security. This department is generally seen as a "heavier," more important department than the CRM, making this change appear to be a political promotion to some. Initiated by a social-democratic under-secretary for Emancipation and administered by a liberal under-secretary, an Emancipation Program for 1985-1990 was presented to and accepted by the Second Chamber in 1986 with many policy initiatives in several areas. One of these areas is the employment of women in the public sector.

Parliamentary Activities

From time to time, the Dutch Second Chamber has explicitly drawn attention to emancipation policy within the civil service as in 1977, when the parliament declared itself in favor of an affirmative action program within the civil service. Ever since a 1979 motion asked for positive action in governmental recruitment policy, recruitment advertisements have been decorated with the following phrase:

> The central government would like to employ more women.
> Therefore, they are especially invited to apply.

The parliament further expanded the application of positive action when it passed a motion requiring the use of positive action to retain greater numbers of women during the implementation of forced retirement policies.

Legal Developments

Since July, 1980, a law on the equal treatment of men and women in civil public service has been in force. According to the first article of this law, authorities are forbidden to discriminate between men and women either directly or indirectly (for instance, by referring to family circumstances or marital status). Exceptions to this rule are allowed only: (1) in cases where the sex of the applicant is directly relevant (e.g., opera singers); (2) to protect women (this concerns primarily rules dealing with pregnancy or motherhood); (3) in cases where one is acting in favor of a certain sex which has been discriminated against in the past. Positive action is legally based upon this article.

Policy Measures

In 1976, a working group for "Emancipation and Part-time Work as Aspects of Governmental Policy" (EDO) was established. The EDO reports showed the need for a structural policy to strengthen the position of women employees. A new committee was formed, the Committee for Internal Emancipation Policy in the Civil Service (CIER), with the special task of translating general emancipation principles into concrete policy measures which could be implemented immediately. Members of the CIER were functionaries dealing with emancipation in the different departments. In due time, three CIER reports were produced concerning three different policy areas.

Report 1: Recruitment and Selection. This CIER report identifies several ways to facilitate the entrance of women into the public service. Recommendations call for changes in function requirements. For most governmental jobs a particular kind of schooling is required. Instead of requiring a certain educational level, the report recommended that the government ask for "function related activities and/or experience." The report suggested that selection committees be mixed as much as possible, on the assumption that a woman applicant will have more self-confidence when a member of her own sex is on a recruitment committee.

A second CIER recommendation in this report was to change the use of absentee statistics to differentiate leaves due to pregnancy from those due to sickness. When both types of leave are conflated, the statistics indicate that women are ill more frequently than men.

Report 2: Training and Education. The CIER recognized that women's participation in departmental training programs should be expanded. The report recommends that in choosing candidates for training, supervisors should discriminate in favor of women. In addition, more training should be provided for those in lower staff positions (where most women are). The report recommends that education occur at appropriate times and that special facilities be created for part-time workers. If possible, childcare ought to be provided. The contents of teaching material should be screened for discriminatory remarks, and where necessary, special (interdepartmental) courses on social skills for women should be established.

Report 3: Career Planning. On the whole, women's careers tend to be less spectacular than men's. Many women never reach the higher echelons of the civil service despite their qualifications. Because pregnancy and motherhood cause women to quit their jobs, CIER recommended an extension of child care facilities, a special kind of career-planning for part-time workers and the development of careers with a built-in break (the Netherlands to date has no extended paternity leaves).

Apart from these three reports, CIER asked for emancipation workers in the different ministries to generate departmental plans, preferably containing *target figures*. By early 1987, five of the thirteen departments had complied with this request. The majority of these plans, however, are plans in preparation and none of them contain target figures. Apart from this, in 1982, all departments were requested to transform 30 percent of their full-time jobs into *part-time work* and an interdepartmental working group began investigating the possibilities for *child care*.

Summarizing, the number and direction of these policy measures reflect considerable goodwill; however, to date, these policies have had very little effect. Part of this is due to the dearth of sanctions available to implement these policies. Unwilling personnel officers can easily ignore all of these policies with impunity.

CONCLUSION

Despite the efforts government has taken to stimulate the entrance and upward mobility of its women employees, the overall figures are not impressive; women administrators, especially in the higher echelons, are still very few in number. Those who started in junior positions experience many barriers to career advancement. One of the more general problems is the existing pattern of gender roles: more than half of the women civil servants who leave their jobs do it for reasons of pregnancy. For those women who pursue a career in public administration, the choice continues to be between career and children. A lack of facilities as well as the negative attitude of personnel officers who are afraid of deviant cases, are both strong barriers in the process of upward mobility for women. As long as departments are unwilling to accommodate the needs of women for more flexible hours and for child care, the position of women will not improve, in spite of the general political climate that supports the hiring of more women.

REFERENCES

Centraal Bureau voor de Statistiek. 1979, 1982. *Statistisch Zakboek*. The Hague: Staatsuitgeverij.
Kring van gemeentesecretarissen in Noord Kennermerland. 1985. *Enquete onder werkneemsters van de gemeente Noord Kennemerland*. The Hague: Ministry of Internal Affairs.

Ministry of Internal Affairs. 1985. *De oorzaak van het verloop onder vrouwen en mannen*. The Hague: Ministry of Internal Affairs.

Ministry of Internal Affairs. 1985. *Emancipatie in Cijfers: 1984*. The Hague: Ministry of Internal Affairs.

Ministry of Internal Affairs. 1989. *Emancipatie in Cijfers: 1988*. The Hague: Ministry of Internal Affairs.

Ministerie van Binnenlandse Zaken. 1984, 1985, 1986, 1989. *De oorzaak van het verloop onder vrouwen en mannen*. The Hague: Ministry of Internal Affairs.

Oudijk, C. 1984. *De Sociale Atlas van de Vrouw*. The Hague: Staatsuitgeverij.

Swiebel, J. 1986. "Het emancipatiebeleid onder het kabinet Lubbers: prelude tot een grote verdwi intruc?" paper presented at the annual meeting of the Dutch Association of Political Science, Amersfoort.

Women in Public Administration in the Federal Republic of Germany

Monika Langkau-Herrmann
Ellen Sessar-Karpp

WOMEN IN THE LABOR FORCE IN WEST GERMANY

Since the end of World War II, women have constituted over one-third of all employed persons in the West German labor force. Women still suffer numerous disadvantages in working life, and their position in the labor market is by no means secure. Women earn 34 percent less than men. Most female blue-collar workers (94 percent) are unskilled or semi-skilled as opposed to only 42 percent of their male colleagues. More than half of all women presently work in only six occupations (office workers, retail clerks, health services, janitorial occupations, agricultural occupations, teachers). Of those women working in industry, commerce, and insurance, 54 percent had no sphere of decision-making or responsibility of their own on the job, as compared to only 15 percent of male employees in these areas. Finally, roughly one-third of all working women have part-time jobs (34 percent in 1983), and two-thirds of all working women report interrupting their employment for family reasons.

WOMEN IN THE PUBLIC SECTOR

The situation of women in the public service in the Federal Republic is particularly significant because the government is one of the most important employers of women and is in a position to set an example for private industry. This article reports on the present status of women in public service in the Federal Republic of Germany as determined from statistical information as well as from a series of empirical investigations by the authors. These include: data from interviews in 1985 with 24 top women administrators in 7 Federal Ministries and in two state authorities, and information gathered in 1981-82 from a survey of 80 women (18 of whom were in the top grade) and 24 men in the public service (Langkau-Herrmann et al. 1983).

Since the beginning of the 1960s, the employment rate for women in the public sector has risen from 25.6 percent to 39 percent in 1983 (in central government service from 17.5 percent in 1960 to 23.9 percent in 1983). As Table 1 indicates, only 16.7 percent of the full-time employees were women and almost half of all women employees worked part-time. Part-time workers are almost entirely female (95 percent).

Women's representation in positions of responsibility and power is very limited (Table 2). Less than one percent of full-time women in the central government service are in the top grade, while only 6.3 percent are in the upper grade.

Only 11 percent of *all* civil servants in the more prestigious central government service are women (Statistische Bundesamt 1983). None of the permanent undersecretaries employed in direct government service are women. Of the 128 heads of subdivisions, only 7 are women, and of the 1963 department heads, only 60 are women (Minister for Home Affairs 1983).

While women are heavily underrepresented in the top grade, promotions for women and opportunities for additional training for the few women in these ranks are the same as for men. Table 3 shows that *in all*

Table 1: Personnel in direct government service 1983

Status	government officials white collar workers blue collar workers	women #	%
full-time employed	1,072,560	179,248	16.7
part-time employed*	84,555	80,358	95.0
part-time employed**	23,827	22,105	92.8
total employed	1,180,942	281,711	23.9

* with at least half of the normal working hours per week.
** with less than half of the normal working hours per week. The labor contracts of the public service exclude part-time workers with less than half of the normal working hours per week.

Source: *Personnel of the government on 30 June 1983*. Wiesbaden.: Statistische Bundesamt.

Table 2: Personnel in federal authorities according to grades

	Total	Women	
		#	%
top grade	6,423	440	6.9
upper grade	6,357	1,090	17.1
middle grade	8,047	4,784	59.5
lower grade	1,623	145	8.9

Source: *Personnel of the government on 30 June 1983.* Wiesbaden:
Statistische Bundesamt.

Table 3: Promotions and career advancements in federal authorities 1980-1983

	Total	Women	
		#	%
top grade	1,715	110	6.4
upper grade	1,684	319	18.9
middle grade	3,056	1,836	60.1
lower grade	605	57	9.4

Source: *Personnel of the government on 30 June 1983.* Wiesbaden:
Statistische Bundesamt.

grades, women's proportion of promotions is about the same as the proportion of women in each grade respectively. Evidence of additional education for women, however, is not as great as women's numbers would warrant in the upper, middle and lower grades (Table 4).

Women in public service continue to bear the main responsibility for family and housework. This, combined with the fact that in the Federal Republic schools are usually in session only in the morning, helps to explain why 95 percent of the part-time employees in the public sector are women. As in the private sector, the jobs for women in the public sector are confined to "typically female" work such as secretarial duties, filing clerk duties, and other monotonous tasks which do not lead to promotions.

Legal Conditions Governing Women's Employment in Public Service

With some exceptions, the legal conditions governing employment and advancement are the same for men and women for all positions in the

Table 4: Participants in further education 1980-1983 in federal authorities

	Total	Women	
		#	%
top grade	3,879	273	7.0
upper grade	3,691	425	11.8
middle grade	2,094	821	39.2
lower grade	405	9	2.2

Source: *Personnel of the government on 30 June 1983.* Wiesbaden: Statistische Bundesamt.

public service. Certain special regulations that are different for men and women govern employment in the customs and police service. Until late 1985, legal leave entitlements for mothers existed for up to 6 months after childbirth and for either parent for up to 5 days per calendar year for caring for a sick child. The Federal Government further facilitated the reconciliation of family duties and gainful employment in January, 1986, by introducing a "child raising leave" which provides that after the eight-week protective period following childbirth, either parent may leave work to care for a child (until the child reaches the age of 12 months) with a job guarantee and a monthly public allowance of DM 600. In addition, the law on part-time work and leave states that civil servants have a right to leave or part-time work (unpaid or reduced pay) up to half of their total working time for up to three years with the possibility of extending the arrangement for up to 9 years for family reasons. This leave can be taken by either the mother or the father.

THE RESEARCH DESIGN

In Spring, 1985, in-depth, open-ended interviews were conducted with a total of 24 women in leading positions in the Federal Ministry of Labor, the Federal Ministry of the Interior, the Federal Ministry for Youth, Family Affairs, Women and Health, the Federal Ministry of Defense, the Federal Ministry of Economics, the Federal Ministry of Finance, the Federal Ministry of Justice, and the Federal Ministry of Foreign Affairs (18 women) as well as two state authorities (6 women). While the heads of departmental sections are not officially counted as management, the small number of women working above this level made it necessary to include heads of departmental sections and above in the sample.

Description of the Sample: Position

Of the 24 women interviewed, 18 held the position of head of a departmental section. Three of the women were heads of a subsection, two were heads of a department, and one woman was in the position of a permanent undersecretary. Only three respondents were able to name women in the ministry above them. Apart from the women working in a position higher than head of departmental section, the female heads of departmental sections were in jobs that emphasized traditionally female activities, such as youth, women, family affairs, and health. Other areas of leadership for women were population policy, labor protection, tax policy, industrial policy, international organizations, and environmental protection. Several women succeeded in ascending via a typical women's department to a department having a higher status.

Description of the Sample:
Age, Marital Status, Education

Only three of the questioned women were younger than 40 years, while 11 were from 40-50 years old. Seven were between 50 and 60, and 3 were over 60. While no statistics exist on the age structure of men and women in management positions in the public service, on the basis of a random-sample survey conducted in two ministries in 1981, three-fourths of all female respondents in the upper grade or top grade, as opposed to two-thirds of the male respondents, were over 40 years of age.

Perhaps the most noticeable difference between men and women in top management positions is the low proportion of married women among the respondents. Only 10 of the 24 women were married (of these, one was separated), two were widowed, two divorced, and the rest were single. Only three women had children under the age of 10 (at the time of the interview), and only 7 had ever had children. These results support those of the 1981 survey which showed that the proportion of married women in the top grade is much lower than the average in public service. (In 1981, 51 percent of all employed women were married.) The majority (78 percent) of the men in the top grade were married, mostly to unemployed women (Langkau-Herrmann et al. 1983, 75).

Schooling and occupational training is an important criterion for access to many careers in the public service. Normally a university degree is the prerequisite for access to the top grade. Especially advantageous for entry to the top grade is a degree in law or economics. The rigid career structure in the public service, especially the inflexible assignment of certain occupational training levels to the individual career groups (lower, middle, upper, and top grade), is responsible for the fact that only in exceptional cases do either male or female employees manage to rise to the next grade by participating in severe test procedures and taking special trainee courses. Experience shows that women are especially disadvantaged in obtaining the access and training prerequisites for the top grade, particularly when the educational requirements stress degrees in law and economics, areas where women have been historically underrepresented.

The women respondents in management positions all had university degrees. Six of them had a doctoral degree. Fourteen studied law and four studied economics. The remainder had degrees in politics, psychology, sociology, and languages.

Professional Development

Almost all of the women in this study had a relatively continuous career in public service. About a third had consciously aspired to their careers. Most identified their motives for the top jobs to be: the wish to create something and carry it through, the desire for professional recognition, the desire to take part in political decision-making, the need to be creative, an interest in planning, organization, and a strong desire for information.

A majority of the women stated that they had taken advantage of all professional opportunities offered to them. They often had advanced by ignoring "well intentioned" advice from their social surroundings that in fact would have hindered their careers. This advice mainly revolved around the fear that a management position would be too great a strain for the women, and that a strong professional commitment would have an unfavorable influence on their private and family lives.

Most women in the sample experienced phases of professional stagnation due to personal or professional factors and did not have careers that developed in a straightforward way. The early death of a husband, or a divorce, caused upheavals in private life which greatly influenced these women's advancement efforts. For women with children, stronger professional commitment became possible only after the children had started to go to school.

Most respondents identified their own personal qualities and motivations as critical to their advancement. For some, managing to obtain particular positions on the career ladder was important. In particular, many women said that the position of head of a departmental section was a milestone in their professional careers, one they had to fight to achieve ("for me it was a question of, to be or not to be"). Another group of respondents credited the improvement in the political climate favoring women for their advancement. A very small group of respondents mentioned support by their superiors as a factor (two of these superiors were women).

Unfair Treatment in Professional Life

A small minority of the respondents claimed that discrimination against women does not exist. These women have fully accepted the male norms, including the ensuing consequences for their private lives. One respondent declared, "If a woman is willing to renounce private and family life in order to commit herself completely to professional life, just like a man, she will have equal opportunities."

Most of the interviewed women, however, indicated that they had experienced or observed discrimination against women in a variety of instances such as during the judgment of performance ("women never receive excellent marks"), during promotion ("too slow, men overtake women in terms of promotion, never the other way around"), and in the reduction of personnel in departments when a woman is put in charge. Discrimination also takes place in the allocation of women to "soft" duties (social, personnel matters) unlike men, who are given more appreciated "hard" duties like economic or financial affairs. In mixed teams, women's ideas and proposals tend to be ignored. During recruitment, many of the female respondents reported being confronted with prejudicial remarks concerning their suitability and aptitude ("this business is too tough," "female superiors are an affront to older employees," or "he does not want a female"). They were warned that they could not perform the required duties of a job in the foreign service or a job involving the testing of men. Finally, married women respondents experienced prejudice against them because of their marital status in that fathers were given precedence at promotion time or they were called a "double wage earner."

More indirectly, women felt discriminated against because the top grade, especially in higher ranks still is a "closed male hierarchy," a "male coterie." The women, however, did not view as discrimination the fact that the government gives little consideration to the life circumstances of women (the problem of family and job).

Many of the women interviewed stated that they had fought against being placed at a disadvantage by talking with superiors and staff council, and in rare cases, by declaring solidarity with women in other departments. Most of the women reported being successful in the use of aggressive methods, several to the extent that they never had to suffer similar handicaps again.

Attitude of Top Women Towards Their Jobs

The women respondents in this study expressed a high degree of job satisfaction. On a scale of one to five with five being "discontent," 19 women responded with a 1 or a 2, and none responded with less than a 3. In explaining this, most of the women mentioned the following as positive factors: the responsibility of the job, the opportunity "to be boss," the high degree of autonomy ("one is in charge of things," "one can get things going"), the opportunity for free creative scope, the opportunity to participate in important decision-making, the opportunity to obtain insights about important political power interests and arrangements. The work motivations for women managers are not significantly different from the work motivations of men with regard to the above characteristics. Male managers did differ from female managers, however, in their ability to offset the disadvantages of having a time consuming, demanding job. Having limited or irregular leisure time and a restricted private life was more difficult for the female managers because of expectations that they also engage in family work. Single female managers complained that they have to pursue their career at the expense of personal relationships. They voice doubts about the value of "renouncing" a happy family life, or whether they "cheated themselves." The married female managers stated that for the sake of private and family life, they did not pursue their professional careers as vigorously as their male colleagues.

Leadership Styles of Women Managers

All of the women interviewed described their leadership style as oriented towards their colleagues and as "democratic." Although they made the final decisions, the women arrived at their decisions after considerable consultation with co-workers. They explained that this process helped to establish a good working climate, motivated male and female colleagues, and ultimately produced good results. The majority of the women interviewed refused to make lone decisions in the form of strict orders and directions, in contrast to their male colleagues whom they felt often exhibited such behavior. The responding women indicated that an authoritarian and impersonal leadership style would not be taken seriously by others. They also expressed a fear of being labelled a hard and bad female boss. Many indicated that the communicative style of leadership has disadvantages. The democratic style may impede the swift accomplishment of duties, especially in an efficiency-oriented organization. Another problem perceived by the respondents is that a democratic style will probably not lead to personal advancement and power as readily as a more demanding leadership style. The female respondents viewed the conflict between the behavioral demands of the hierarchy ("ability to assert oneself," "swift execution of duties," "efficiency") and female role expectations ("friendly behavior of women," "avoidance of aggressive behavior towards co-workers"), not as a structural problem, but as a result of their own personal weaknesses. Some women critically characterized their own work style as "having too much patience."

In contrast, the female managers favorably viewed male colleagues as having a rational and pragmatic work style that serves to accomplish tasks and assists career advancement. The women criticized some aspects of male work style, such as, (1) having an excessive desire to stand out, and (2) ruthlessly striving to advance one's career often without regard either for the purpose of the work or for the consequences to partners.

The respondents identified clear differences between men and women at the same professional level in the methods used to make presentations. The women describe themselves and other women in high level jobs as expressing their arguments in strictly objective and precise language. They do not see this behavior as typical for their male colleagues of the same rank who often speak without making well-founded contributions ("they are allowed to do this more than women").

Women in leading positions are still in an exceptional situation and are fully aware of this status. They weigh their words and decisions, because they know that they are especially visible and that their words and behavior must withstand strong critical examination. Because the behavioral norms of the bureaucracy are primarily male ("to push one's way," "to aim at maximum performance of co-workers"), women in high-level positions combine male norms with friendly presentations or sometimes even a motherly attitude to develop their own individual behavioral patterns. Women managers consequently exhibit a broader range of styles than is the case for men.

Many of the women had a skeptical or even negative attitude towards the leadership style within their organizations. The main shortcomings are, in their view, the making of major decisions too high in the hierarchy and the unreasonably strict regulation of responsibilities according to rules of procedure, with insufficient consideration being given to skills and abilities. The female respondents often noted that they bypass the formal hierarchical channels occasionally. They view their male colleagues as being much more conformist with regard to hierarchical structures and procedures. The women view men as better at using a given hierarchy for their own professional advancement. They are better able to oppose unreasonable demands from outside and to pass on duties which do not lie in their area of activity. In general, women in leading positions demonstrate only minimal adjustment to hierarchical structures. This hinders women's professional advancement.

To learn more about the specific attitudes of women in high level positions towards competition and conflict, each respondent was asked whether she had a peaceful and cooperative work situation and/or whether she sometimes felt that the work situation resembled a battlefield. The reaction was highly varied. A fairly large number of the women interviewed felt that a peaceful workplace is desirable, but work without conflict is unrealistic. The golden mean is ideal, but "if the matter itself demands it," "if it is a matter affecting your very position," one should not avoid conflicts and should attempt to prevail in the face of resistance. A small number of women stressed that they enjoy confrontation and struggle, that peaceful cooperation is dull for them, and that given a peaceful work situation, they would probably try to find another job. An even smaller group of respondents reported feeling at ease only in a harmonious work environment. They would forgo an interesting position instead of accepting fierce struggles and confrontation. These few women openly indicated that they have problems coping with male competition. Overall, however, most of the women indicated that they readily compete and conflict with male counterparts, at least in cases where they deem it necessary.

WOMEN'S NETWORKS

To ascertain whether women who are a minority in male dominated higher echelons of public bureaucracies have access to the more informal circles of their colleagues of equal or higher rank, the women respondents were asked whether they interact with a circle of persons who help them in their professional advancement.

Only four respondents gave a spontaneously affirmative answer to this question: one of them referred expressly to an otherwise purely male circle of acquaintances, while the others mostly referred to purely female contacts in several public authorities. The women in question all know each other personally and provide mutual help with professional queries.

About one-third of the respondents stressed that they merely cultivate loose contacts with women in similar professional positions within the same public authority and/or with other public bodies. However, these women replied that they furnished mutual professional support and information, if necessary, but they avoided the idea of a network of professional contacts. They interpreted such an arrangement as too rigid and formalized. Another third of the respondents admitted to having a strong feeling of togetherness with other women, but shrank from common actions of solidarity designed to improve their professional situation.

Three of the respondents belong to a group of women who meet at regular intervals in a restaurant but who attach greater importance to the social rather than the professional aspects of these meetings.

A small minority of the women stated that they do not maintain any informal contacts with their colleagues, either male or female, outside of required professional contacts. This attitude is prevalent among women in completely male-dominated sectors where "everyone fights her/his own battles," as one woman stated.

Occasionally, the interviews revealed that some women deliberately avoid closer contacts with other women of equal rank — especially those from the same public authority ("Anything but that!"). They shun the manifest appearance of these contacts at work, not to avoid professional competition with other women but, because they fear the defensive reactions of equal and more senior colleagues. They worry that belonging to a female clique might put them in the wrong corner and make them seem ridiculous, a position that would lead to setbacks in professional advancement. A comparison of surveys performed in 1981 and 1985 on this question shows that in recent years even women in very senior positions have become more conscious of their own professional isolation in a unilaterally male-shaped work environment (Langkau-Herrmann et al. 1983).

Social gatherings occur in most departments on the occasion of birthdays and promotions. Most respondents, however, do not like such events because they "have no time for them" or they believe that "too much celebration takes place." Apparently, the isolation of women in top ranks emerges with particular clarity during informal meetings, situations which generate uncertainty on both sides.

MENTORING ACTIVITIES BY WOMEN

The literature on this subject provides very different answers to the question of how much women in high positions act to help other women, both to participate in leading functions and decisions and to advance professionally (Schein 1975, 343). V.E. Schein believes that isolated women in top positions are so pressured to adjust to male power structures that they, like their male counterparts, decide in favor of men with regard to the selection of applicants, promotion, and the distribution of tasks (Schein 1975, 343). The overwhelming majority of women respondents declared that they often had opportunities during their professional activities to give support to other women in their own public authorities. Furthermore, they were able to name a wide range of supportive measures. These ranged from giving personal advice and help to arranging talks with superiors and colleagues about work-related questions (such as further vocational training and advanced instruction, promotion, transfer, part-time work, formulation of applications, relations with colleagues, and information about the public authority in question). Over half of the respondents stated that they either initiated or took part in the development of measures which are of interest to women such as establishing a women's section in their own public authority, developing guidelines for the promotion of women, and founding women's advice centers.

With regard to personnel decisions, the results are less clear. A small minority of women stated that they had systematically pursued a policy of recruitment and promotion in favor of women. For this, they report having been criticized by superiors and management ("you seem to want to engage women only"). Furthermore, they recognized that if ultimately successful, this policy could result in a certain devaluation of their own work (a women's department). Most of the women respondents favored a balanced blend of male and female colleagues. The women believed that such a blend would help balance the working styles of both males and females. Some respondents worried about having women constitute too big a portion of a department or section. A minority of the respondents preferred male colleagues, at least during the development phase of their tasks, because they felt that men had greater prestige and were more assertive. In general, most women report themselves to be torn between female solidarity and the male-oriented criteria governing the selection and evaluation of applicants in personnel matters. Only a minority of the respondents had been able to evade the constraints that mitigate against the hiring of female applicants to any large degree.

FACTORS HINDERING OR ASSISTING CAREER ADVANCEMENT

The interviewees identified far more factors hindering the advancement of women than factors assisting such advancement. Among the most often mentioned obstacles were: (1) family commitments; (2) lack of self confidence; (3) lack of desire for advancement; (4) the preponderance of men in certain areas of work and at the upper echelons of the bureaucracy; (5) the division of men's jobs and women's jobs into "hard" and "easy"; (6) the male dominated administrative culture; (7) the attitude of the administration towards female employees; and (8) the old boy's network.

In discussing the factors assisting the career advancement of women, some of the women questioned were unable to name any. The following factors were mentioned by a minority in each case: (1) the growing proportion of women in the public sector; (2) the growing competence, aptitude, education, and training of women; (3) the development of an old girl's network; (4) the increasing participation by women in political parties and trade unions; and (5) the growing women's movement in the Federal Republic of Germany.

CONCLUSIONS

Women in management positions in the public service constitute a minority of around 1 percent at the very highest grade, and no more than 6 percent at the upper grade. They operate in a workforce where role conflict for working women with children is very high. Part-time work for women is a very common practice, and fewer women than men obtain higher education. Because of their minority status, women are pressured to adapt to labor structures determined by men. In their advancement endeavors and in their treatment of co-workers, top women managers often develop their own behaviors and strategies which distinguish them not only from women in typically female professions, but also from men in similar positions. Most of the responding women have consciously decided to use a cooperative and communicating style of leadership, which they see as a major precondition for motivating subordinates and achieving a satisfactory working climate. They reject an impersonal management style but realize that through these working methods they are limiting themselves and renouncing important power resources that their positions offer them in a hierarchically organized authority. Most respondents viewed their female behaviors as personal weaknesses rather than as structural contradictions or positive assets.

To overcome the isolation women in high management positions experience, women's networks have served as a counterbalance to the male-dominated informal circles and professional organizations which largely exclude women. In the organizations visited in this study, women's networks appear in only rudimentary form. While many women in management positions realize the need for mutual support, these same women are very cognizant of the negative retaliation that such networks might evoke from male colleagues. In general, most who participate in any semblance of a network do so with caution.

Data from this study indicate that West German women in leading positions, unlike their male colleagues, experience role conflicts and are less likely to adapt to hierarchical structures. This partly hinders their own career progress. However, the more detached attitude of women towards traditional administrative structures is a potential source of change. Were top women no longer an exceptional phenomenon and consequently under no pressure to conform to dominant male norms, women at the top could act to improve the employment conditions for other lower ranking women. With no more than 6 percent in the upper grades, women do not yet constitute a critical mass. They must continue to behave in carefully prescribed ways if they are to maintain their high positions.

STRATEGIES FOR CHANGE

To achieve greater female participation in management positions in the public service, profound changes must occur in society as well as in the governmental bureaucracies. Perhaps the most important and difficult of these is changing the sex specific division of labor which women identify as the main source of discrimination against women in employment. The public service gears recruitment and promotion to the model of the male employee who is often free from family tasks (mostly because of an unemployed wife). Not only must the distribution of family roles be changed, but a social consciousness of the fundamental importance of family duties, especially child-raising work, must be fostered and incorporated into law and in labor contracts for the public service. The norm of the child care-free male employee must be abandoned.

As short term strategies, greater female participation in management positions could be obtained through: (1) giving preference to female applicants in jobs where women have been underrepresented; (2) altering career ladder requirements that discriminate against women; (3) motivating women to obtain training in typical female areas; (4) using affirmative action plans to advance women into key positions; and (5) passing an anti-discrimination act that punishes violations with effective sanctions. These are but a sample of some of the strategies that deserve attention.

REFERENCES

Langkau-Herrman, M., J. Langkau, R. Weinert, R. Nejedlo. 1983. *Frauen im öffentlichen Dienst.* Bonn: Verlag Neue Gesellschaft.

Minister for Home Affairs. 1983. Unpublished manuscript.

Schein, V.E. 1975. "Relationship Between Sex Role Stereotypes and Requisite Management Characteristics Among Female Managers." *Journal of Applied Psychology v.* 60, n. 3.

Statistische Bundesamt. 1983. *Personal des Bundes am 30 Juni 1983.* Weisbaden:

Women in Public Administration in Finland

Sirkka Sinkkonen
Eva Hänninen-Salmelin

WOMEN IN THE LABOR FORCE

Finnish women have a long history of participation in the labor force. In 1890, in Helsinki, about 39 percent of all working age women were in paid labor. By 1900, this figure had grown to 55 percent (Jallinoja 1983, 225). In the whole country, 32 percent of women in the non-agricultural population participated in the labor force in 1900 and 39 percent in 1920 (Haavio-Mannila 1980, 11). In 1983, 73 percent of all working age women were in the labor force, and almost half (48 percent) of the total labor force consisted of women (Central Statistical Office 1985, 116).

In 1987, one-fourth of the total Finnish labor force (over 659,000 of the 4.9 million total population) was employed by the public sector. Two-thirds of these (about 448,000) worked in the municipalities and their federations and one-third (about 211,000) worked with the state. The public sector, especially the municipalities, is a large employer of women. Almost half (42 percent) of the female, but only 25 percent of the male, labor force is in the public sector. The large municipal sector is dominated by women; 75 percent of its permanent monthly salaried employees are women. In contrast, 60 percent of the state employees are men (Central Statistical Office 1985, 23).

Within both the public and the private economies, the gender distribution of employees varies according to function. In Finland, the public sector involves the functions of the state and the municipalities and is involved with a variety of direct services to the people such as providing preventive and curative health care, education, children's day care, social security, and other welfare services, as well as with activities that support the basic infrastructure of the society, such as construction and maintenance of roads, highways, and bridges; the rail, energy, and post and telecommunication services. The major areas of employment in the pri-

69

vate sector, where 75 percent of the workers are male, are in industry, business, commerce, insurance, and banking. Males also dominate state-run employment areas such as transportation services, roads, highways, police, and the army. Among state employees, only within the post and telecommunication services are women included. In contrast, the municipal sector has a high proportion of women because the municipalities and their federations are responsible for the traditionally female functions of health and social services, primary and secondary school services, and part of vocational education.

Women have not always dominated the Finnish public sector. Finnish women first entered state employment on a permanent basis in 1864 in the General Directorate of Post and Telecommunication services. Despite this early entrance, the number of women in the state public sector (the municipal sector had not yet developed) was relatively small when compared to the relatively high labor force participation of women. Career opportunities in the state were opened gradually for women partially through the granting of exemptions and partly through the issuance of statutes (Koskinen 1982). The first women entered state service in 1864 by exemption. The first statute to open some offices in the post and telecommunication services was enacted in 1881, and was followed by a series of other similar statutes towards the end of the century. In 1885, women statutorily achieved access to teaching positions in girls' schools. In 1897 came the statute permitting women to function as physicians. The statute granting women access to lecturers' jobs in women's colleges, and the statute allowing women to function as clerks (kanslisti, a supporting administrative job) in the National Board of Education were enacted in 1898 (Koskinen 1982).

While some public offices were formally opened to women at the end of the last century, these positions were restricted for a long time to unmarried women and to low level positions. No women were permitted to hold responsible public positions until 1926. One restriction provided that married women be allowed to handle public or private money only if their husbands would assume financial responsibility for that money (Huhtanen 1983, 101). This law remained in effect until 1930. As the economy became more industrialized and the demand for labor increased, women were recruited into the public service to perform increasingly repetitious and low paying jobs in the areas of collecting, handling, transmitting, and storing information, accounting, auditing, and bookkeeping. This served to further differentiate and sex segregate the public sector labor force.

THE CURRENT REPRESENTATION OF WOMEN
IN THE FINNISH POLITICAL SYSTEM
AND IN PUBLIC ADMINISTRATION

As Figure 1 shows, the legislative power in Finland is vested in the parliament whose 200 members are elected every four years by direct, secret, and proportional ballot. In the parliamentary elections in 1982, 32 percent of the 200 MPs elected were women. The highest position ever held by a woman in the Finnish political-administrative system is the first vice chairperson of the Finnish Parliament, an office held by a woman for the first time during 1975-1979.

The President of the Republic and the Council of State (the Cabinet) have the highest executive authority. Finland has never had a woman either as president or as prime minister. The small Liberal party ran the first woman presidential candidate in the election of 1982.

Due to the specific historical development of Finland, Finnish government combines ministerial departments and central boards. The 20 central boards, also called national boards, are remnants of Swedish rule which lasted until 1809. The ministries (now 13 in number) came from the period when Finland was under Russian rule (until 1917) and have their roots in the French type of ministerial system. These two types of agencies with 3,229 employees in the ministries and 5,791 employees in the national boards constituted the total personnel in central state employment in 1984. The total number of personnel in state employment in 1984 was about 210,000.

In 1987, the ministries had 16 ministers because three of the ministries had two ministers (education, finance, and health and social welfare). Four of the 16 were women. They were the ministers of education, health, and the interior. Finland's first woman minister was Miina Sillanpaa, a minister of social affairs from the Social Democratic Party in 1926-27. A second woman minister was not appointed until 1944. She was Hertta Kuusinen from the Communist Party and without a portfolio. The last Finnish Cabinet without a woman minister was appointed in 1966 and sat until 1968. Since then, Finland has always had one to four women ministers. Most of the women ministers have been in only two ministries, those of education and social affairs and health, both traditional women's role areas. Occasionally, women have presided also over the ministries of agriculture and finance. The ministries of commerce and industry, justice, and interior have had a woman minister only once. The ministries of defense, traffic, foreign affairs, labor, and environment have never had a woman minister (Skard and Haavio-Mannila 1985).

In addition to the ministers who are political leaders, each ministry also has a permanent bureaucratic chief. These 13 highest civil servants in Finland have always been men. In the mid-1980s, only one woman was in

FIGURE 1. Structure of public administration in Finland

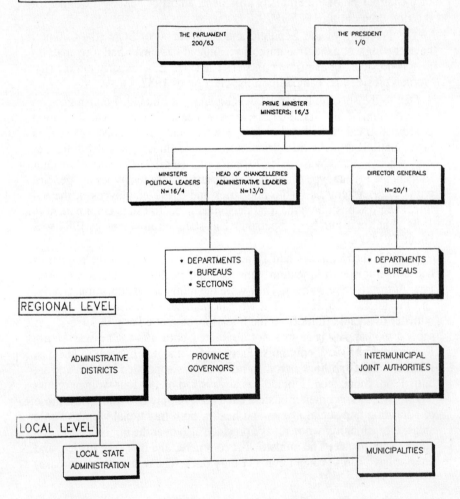

the second highest level of the civil service which includes the 20 director-generals of the 20 administrative national boards. She was in the National Board of Social Welfare, which has had a tradition of having a female director-general since the 1960s. All other national boards have always been headed by men. Directly under the chiefs of the ministries and the national boards are the heads of the departments. Under them are the heads of the bureaus and, in some ministries, the heads of the sections or divisions (See Figure 1).

At the department head level, which is the third highest level in the hierarchy, two of the 61 department heads were women in 1986. One of these women headed the Department of Research in the ministry of Health and Social Affairs from 1968 to 1987 when she retired due to age and was replaced by a man. The other woman has headed the Department of Physical Planning and Construction in the new Ministry of Environment since 1985. In 1986, 4 of the 30 assistant department heads were women (11 percent). Of the 161 heads of bureaus, 15 were women (9 percent), and of the 12 assistant heads of bureaus, 5 were women (42 percent). This same pattern of declining women's representation in the higher echelons of the hierarchy characterizes the administrative national boards as well.

At the regional level, the Finnish public sector has three types of administrative structures. First, the country is divided into 12 provinces each having its own provincial government for general administration. Second, many branches of state government have developed their own administrative structure for occupational safety and labor. Finally, the third type of structure consists of intermunicipal joint authorities with their own decision-making bodies such as the councils, boards, and directorates. These are part of municipal local self government and do not belong to the state bureaucracy as do the first two structures mentioned above. These joint municipal authorities (also called federation of communes) are in some cases required by law and in some cases based on voluntary collaboration among municipalities. They are mostly responsible for running the highly specialized hospital and health services, and in some cases, primary health care and vocational training. The municipalities provide primary health care. The 12 provincial boards are responsible for the general development of the province and have administrative functions with regard to tax administration, the police, monetary transactions of the state, educational and health services, social security, and the supervision of the municipalities. The provincial boards are headed by the Governor of the Province. Turku and Pori Province has twice had a woman as Governor since 1972. The remaining governors are all men. Only since 1972 has it been legally possible to appoint a woman to this position.

The provincial governments are also divided into departments and bureaus. Here again, where the majority of workers are women, the bureaucracy is run mainly by men. Among the 31 department heads were 3 women (10 percent in 1984). One had been in the Department of Health and Social Welfare in the Kuopio Province since 1980, and two were in the provinces of Central Finland (since 1978), and North Carelia (since 1981). Among the 65 bureau chiefs, five were women (8 percent) in 1984.

At the local level, in addition to the municipalities (461 in 1987), many branches of the state administration have their own local administrative units such as the police, post and telecommunication services, the state rail, employment offices, and social security offices. These local agencies are part of the state bureaucracy and do not belong to the municipal public administration.

Women are also absent from the higher administrative positions in the local self-government system. Only 7 municipalities out of 461 had a woman as municipal director in 1985. This number increased to 8 in 1987, all of which were in rural areas. In 1990, 5 women were assistant directors in large cities. The municipal director is the highest official in the municipal public bureaucracy. In spite of the fact that about 75 percent of the monthly salaried municipal workers are women, the men head the municipal departments, offices, and boards (Sinkkonen 1985).

AN EMPIRICAL STUDY OF THE PERCEPTIONS OF WOMEN ADMINISTRATORS

The data on which this report is based were collected partly using structured interviews, and partly using mail questionnaires containing open-ended and structured questions developed by the international project methodology. Twenty-five women administrators from the highest positions in the Finnish central administration responded both to the questionnaire and the interview. All respondents were in the position of bureau head or above in the Finnish central (national) level administration. Table 1 describes the sample of women selected for this study by listing the number of all leading civil servants, the number of all leading women civil servants, and the number of women interviewed for this study according to ministry or national administrative board.

The 25 women and 18 male administrators in our study represent the following ministries and national administrative boards according to their positions.

Heads of department in ministries.	Ministry of Health and Social Affairs Ministry of Environment
Assistant heads of department in ministries.	Ministry of Health and Social Affairs Ministry of Education Ministry of Trade and Commerce
Heads of department in national boards.	National Board of Health National Board of Social Welfare National Board of Vocational Education
Assistant heads of department in national board	National Board of Social Welfare National Board of Vocational Education National Board of Trade and Commerce Interests
Head of bureau in ministries.	Ministry of Education Ministry of Labor Ministry of the Environment Ministry for Foreign Affairs Ministry of Trade and Industry Ministry of Finance Ministry of International Affairs
Head of bureau in national board.	National Board of Social Welfare National Board of Trade and Commerce Interests National Board of Patent and Registration National Board of Forestry National Board of Customs National Board of Health National Board of Waters

The gender segregation is also visible among the top level administrators in the Finnish state bureaucracy. Most of these women represent the fields of health, social affairs, and education (Rose 1976, 247-289; Sinkkonen and Haavio-Mannila 1981, 195-215; Hernes and Hänninen-Salmelin 1985, 111). The Ministries of Defense and Interior, which are the core areas of the state bureaucracy, have no women in higher administrative positions.

Table 1: Description of the Women Administrators in this Study

Positions	Total 1983	Women 1983	Interviewed 1985 Women	1987 Men
Chancelleries of ministries	13	0	0	0
Director-generals of national boards	20	1	0	0
Department heads in ministries	56	2	2	1
Assistant department heads in ministries	31	2	2	2
Department heads in central boards	43	2	2	1
Asst. department heads in central boards	34	4	4	0
Bureau heads in ministries	134	9	9	7
Bureau heads in central boards	235	47	6	7
Other managers	132	15	-	0
Total	698	82 (12%)	25	18

BACKGROUND INFORMATION OF THE INTERVIEWED WOMEN ADMINISTRATORS: AGE AND EDUCATION

The women administrators in the sample represent different age groups. Several (16 percent) were near retirement and reflected views quite different from their younger colleagues, 28 percent of whom were between the ages of 33 and 39. Table 2 shows the age of the women at the time of the last appointment and at the time of the interview. The majority (56 percent) of the interviewed women administrators were appointed to their present offices when they were 40-49 years old and a third of them were appointed during the ages of 33-39.

All of the women administrators in the study had an academic degree which is required to enter the public service as an analyst or senior official. Six (24 percent) of the women and 4 (16 percent) of the men had two degrees. The female administrators have a slightly higher level of education than the male administrators. A study of the highest officials in Finland performed in 1983 determined that 22 percent of this group (both men and women) had a doctor's or a licenciate level degree (Volanen 1983, 239). In this study of women administrators, 24 percent had these

Table 2. The Age of Women Administrators at the time of their Last Appointment and at the Time of the Interview

Age	Last Appointment				At Interview			
	Women		Men		Women		Men	
	#	%	#	%	#	%	#	%
33-39	10	40	11	44	7	28	1	4
40-49	12	48	13	52	7	24	12	4
50-59	3	12	1	4	8	32	10	40
60 & over	-	-	-	-	4	16	2	8
Total	25	100	25	100	25	100	18	100
Youngest-Oldest	32-57		30-50		33-64		38-61	

higher degrees in comparison with 16 percent of the men. Table 3 details the educational background of the administrators interviewed for this study.

Finland is one of the few countries where a university degree is a formal requirement for appointment to the civil service (Modeen 1983, 11-12). When the office involves general administrative functions, the degree is not specified but in other cases (expertise functions) a certain degree is required. Requirements for the leading offices are defined by law.

As might be expected according to other studies of public administrators in Finland (Heiskanen and Sinkkonen 1974; Volanen 1983, 238; Stalhberg 1983, 95-96), most (40 percent) of the women interviewed for this study had a law degree. The second most frequent field in the sample was political science with Ph.D., Licenciate or Master's degrees. Three women in our data (12 percent) had a degree in engineering, which is quite rare among women in Finland. These women have already broken some barriers in obtaining their educational degrees. Three of the respondents had a lower degree in economics prior to pursuing a higher degree in law, political science, or engineering. In summary, the data indicate that both the choice of educational field and the level (academic or vocational) is an extremely important factor determining women's possibilities for advancement in public administration. Entry and promotion in public administration is possible without a university degree, but such exemptions are rare and more often granted to men rather than women (for instance, in the ministry for foreign affairs). Although education is necessary, it is not a sufficient requirement for career advancement in the Finnish public service.

Table 3: Educational Background of Interviewed Finnish Administrators

Level of Education

	Women		Men	
	#	%	#	%
Ph.D. degree	2	8	3	12
Licenciate degree (between MA & PhD)	4	16	1	4
Master's or Bachelor's degree	19	76	22	88
Total	25	100	25	100

Field of Education in Highest Degree*

	#	%	#	%
Law	10	40	10	40
Political Science & Social Sciences (2 PhDs)	8	32	5	20
Engineering				
Humanities	3	12	4	25
Mathematics	2	8	2	8
Forestry	1	4	2	8
Medicine	1	4	-	-
	-	-	2	8
Total	25	100	25	100

* 3 women had lower degrees in economics and 3 men had two degrees, one of which was in economics

Career Histories and Job Satisfaction

When asked for their reasons for entering a career in public administration (see Table 4), 32 percent (8 of the 25 women) and 64 percent of the men (16 of the 25) indicated their educational backgrounds were responsible for their interest in the public service. Two women and three men had Ph.D. degrees; four women and one man had Licenciate degrees (a degree between the Ph.D. and the Master's degree) and all had a Master's degree. Twenty percent of the women (5) and 28 percent of the men (7) mentioned the characteristics of public administration as a reason for entering. Four women said that their entry into public administration as a career was the result of accidental situational factors. One woman revealed an active choice on her part to reject her originally planned university career. When she saw how women were treated in the appointment of professors, she realized that as a woman she would not have an opportunity for a career at the university. She left the university.

A third of the women had special reasons for entering public adminis-

Table 4: Reasons for Entering Public Administration

	Women		Men	
	#	%	#	%
*Appropriate educational background, interest in social affairs, asked to enter because of education	8	32	16	64
*Characteristics of public administration-- interesting functions, active recruitment process, safety, and many career opportunities	5	20	7	28
*By chance, the result of accidental situational factors, because of life situation, open position available	3	12	2	8
*Special reasons for women: -Opportunities for equal payment(5) -Better career mobility (4) -facilitates career and work better (4)	8	32	-	-
Total	25	100	25	100

tration. They considered public administration jobs to be secure and risk-less for women. The regular and often shorter working hours in the public sector facilitated combining career and family. Pensions were also a factor. The public sector was offering pensions of about 60 percent of monthly salaries at the time when the oldest of the interviewed women entered the public service. The private sector offered no such pension at that time, although it currently does.

The majority of the women mentioned that another person had served as an example or had an influence on the formation of their view of public administration. The women had more reasons for entering public administration than did their male colleagues, whose responses centered mainly on education and work experience. The issue of salary was mentioned as a positive factor for entry among the women but as a deterrent among the men.

In evaluating their jobs, the women reported enjoying independent, demanding work where creativity is possible. They disliked bureaucratic structures and bureaucratic processes. About half of both the male and the female respondents reported that they were planning to seek a higher position. The arguments for not seeking advancement given by men and women differ. More women mentioned self development, while men emphasized salary and promotion.

While the women who were interviewed did not mention the impact of role modeling on their career choices, most of the women administrators had very well-educated parents. When age is taken into consideration, both the mothers and the fathers of the respondents had educational attainments much above the average level of the population in general. Also, many of the mothers of these women had rather independent occupations other than that of housewife and mother.

In summary, about one-third of the women considered their jobs in public administration to be secure and riskless for women. Furthermore, the regular and often shorter working hours in the public sector make combining paid with family work an easier task. Pensions were also a factor. The public sector was offering pensions of about 60 percent of monthly salaries at the time these women entered the public service. The private sector offered no pensions.

When asked to evaluate their current job, 68 percent of the women said that they were satisfied or very satisfied and 24 percent (6) were only somewhat satisfied. Nine women reported that they were planning to seek a higher position and 15 (60 percent) said that they would not seek advancement. Those seeking to advance desired more demanding tasks or wanted an opportunity to develop themselves. One person stated: "I have done these tasks long enough, I am ready for the next appointment." When asked to evaluate their own opportunities for advancement, only one woman felt her chances to be good. All the other women either did not know or rated their chances as poor. This pessimism may not reflect any perceived bias against women. The respondents were not optimistic about anyone's opportunities for career advancement in public administration in general. Over half stated that opportunities are poor for everyone. The reasons the 15 respondents gave for not desiring a higher position involved primarily age and current job satisfaction. Four of the fifteen said that they did not desire a higher position because they never would be selected.

Factors Helping or Hindering Women's Advancement in Public Administration

When asked to identify factors which had been most important in hindering women's advancement in public administration, the men more often than the women mentioned the personal characteristics of women and women's lack of qualities required in management positions. When asked about factors that have helped women advance, men most often mentioned women's personal characteristics once again. The women when asked to respond to the same questions also mentioned their own personal characteristics, their skill, and their competence; however, the women were much more likely also to mention structural factors such as the nominating process, recruitment practices, and the masculine tradition as barriers to their own advancement. As factors helping women, women cited changes in the social environment and in women's life situations, changes in the characteristics of public administration, and especially changes in women's own preparation, education, and motivation as important.

The women who currently hold relatively high positions in the Finnish state administration view their own success and the success of the other women as due primarily to individual personal characteristics. Like the male administrators, they consider individual performance the main reason for success and also the primary reason for failure.

Within the workplace, most of the women in the sample (83 percent) did not belong to any women's organizations or networks and most (78 percent) did not belong to any women's professional organizations either. The respondents were somewhat more active in women's organizations in the community as only 65% stated that they did not belong to any women's organizations in their communities.

Present Marital and Family Roles

The data in this study support the findings of other studies of men and women in top administrative positions in Finland that fewer women than men are married (Haavio-Mannila 1981; Sinkkonen and Hänninen 1978; Vanhala 1986; Karento 1987). Just over half of the female administrators in this study were married; however 94 percent of the male administrators were married (see Table 5).

Eleven women administrators in this study had no children. Fourteen had 2, 3, and 4 children; for a total of 34 children. Only two of the children were under 10 years old and only four were under 20 years old. Seven of the children, however, live at home and help with the household

Table 5: Marital Status of Female and Male Administrators

Marital Status	Women		Men	
	#	%	#	%
Unmarried	6	24	0	0
Married or cohabiting	13	52	17	94
Living separately or divorced	5	20	1	5
Widowed	3	12	0	0
Total	25	100	18	100

work. The women administrators in top positions in Finland had spouses with leadership positions in the public or private sectors. Eighty percent of the married women had husbands with a Master's degree or higher.

CONCLUSIONS

The overall picture of women in public administration in Finland is one in which women dominate the lower level offices as well as offices in certain fields within the state and municipal administration, with only a few token leadership positions at the department head level and above in national boards and ministries. Only at the bureau head level on the national boards do women occupy as many as 20 percent of the positions. At the level of planning, preparing, and implementing the laws, statutes, and regulations, women's participation varies from 15 percent to 60 percent according to the field of administration. Women are poorly represented in the higher administrative positions despite the fact that women are well represented in the pool from which persons are recruited for higher positions.

The relationship between the political decision-making system and the administrative system is constantly changing; the relationship has become more reciprocal based on the new type of frame-laws. These new laws often define the future guidelines for certain state functions and allocate the financial resources for many subsequent years. These new frame-laws enhance the power of high civil servants as implementors. Ministers and the political parties recognize this and the recruitment of senior civil service officials has come to involve party politics.

The women administrators in our data are well-educated, hard-working, and aware of the societal, political and structural barriers to their advancement, the factors which facilitate their careers, and their own characteristics. They have a realistic view of what they can do in their own work to help other women and are especially aware of the ways that public policies impact on women. The women administrators report working to generate more opportunities for women in lower offices. They also work to develop open and informal working environments. Top women administrators in Finland are satisfied with their jobs. They are as ambitious as their male colleagues. Whereas top male administrators respond to questions about motivation and advancement in a rather traditional one dimensional way involving salaries and promotions, female administrators have more complex reasons and motives for doing what they do. In their quest, they are articulating new challenges not only for themselves but also for the development of public administration as a whole.

REFERENCES

Central Statistical Office (CSO). 1984. *Naisten asema.* (Position of Women) Helsinki: Central Statistical Office.

Central Statistical Office. 1985. Naiset ja miehet työelämässä (Women and men in worklife). Helsinki: Central Statistical Office, N. 116.

Eriksson, Alina. 1937. "Naiset Posti-ja lennätinlaitoksen palveluksessa" (Women in Post and Telecommunication) in Koskimies, Einari (ed). Helsinki: Posti-ja lennätinlaitos. 229-235.

Haavio-Mannila, Elina. 1980. "Changes in the Life Patterns of Families in the Nordic Countries." *Yearbook of Population Research in Finland XVII.* Helsinki: The Population Research Institute.

Haavio-Mannila, Elina *et.al.* (eds). 1981. *Unfinished Democracy: Women in Nordic Politics.* Elmsford, N.Y.: Pergamon Press.

Haavio-Mannila, Elina. 1981. "The Position of Women." In *Nordic Democracy,* eds. Erik Allardt et. al. Copenhagen: The Danish Society.

Hänninen-Salmelin, Eva. 1987. Postimestarin leskestä pääjohtajaksi-vaiheita virkanaisten urakehityksestä (From Postmaster's widow to Chief Director – Phases in Female Civil Servants' Careers). In *Tulen kesyttäjät.* (Tamers of Fire). The Finnish Federation of University Women. Porvoo: Werner Söderström Osakeyhtiö 157-173.

Heiskanen, Ilkka, and Sirkka Sinkkonen. 1974. From Legalism to Information Technology and Politization: The Development of Public Administration. Helsinki: Research Report, Institute of Political Science, University of Helsinki, N. 31.

Hernes, Helga, and Eva Hänninen-Salmelin. 1985. "Women in the Corporate System." In *Unfinished Democracy: Women in Nordic Politics,* eds. Elina Haavio-Mannila et. al. Elmsford, N.Y.: Pergamon Press.

Huhtanen, Raija. 1983. "Naisen virkakelpoisuuden historiallista tarkastelua" (Women and the Requirements for Office from the Historical Perspective). Tampere Oikeus: Suomen Demokradtt iset lakimichet ja Oikeus-ja yhteiskuntatieteellinen yhdistys 2, 93-104.

Jallinoja, Riita. 1983. Miehet ja naiset (Men and Women). In Sualmalaiset (Finns), eds. T. Valkonen et al. Porvoo: Werner Söderström Osakeyhtiö, 222-250.

Karento, Helena. 1987. "Naiset Hallintoviroissa" (Women in higher civil service). Unpublished manuscript.

Koskinen, Pirkko K. 1982. "Oikeustieteen normit ja naisen todellisuus" (Legal Norms and Woman's Reality). In *Toisenlainen tasa-arvo* (Different Reality), eds. Sirkka Sinkkonen and Eila Ollikainen. Pieksämäli: Kustannuskiila Oy. 89-96.

Modeen, Tor ed. 1983. "Recruiting for High Offices in the Central Administration." Tampere: Department of Administrative Sciences. International Institute of Administrative Sciences, University of Tampere. N. 2/A.

Rose, Richard. 1976. "On the Priorities of Government: A Development Analysis of Public Policies." *European Journal of Political Research.* N. 4. 247-289.

Sinkkonen, Sirkka. 1977. "Women's Increased Political Participation in Finland: Real Influence or Pseudodemocracy?" Berlin: European Consortium for Political Research.

Sinkkonen, Sirkka. 1982. "Naisjohtaja johtaa toisin" (Women leaders lead differently). In *Toisenlainen tasa-arvo* (Different Equality), eds. Sirkka Sinkkonen and Eila Ollikainen. Kuopio: Kustannuskiila.

Sinkkonen, Sirkka. 1985. "Women in Local Politics." In *Unfinished Democracy: Women in Nordic Politics,* eds. Elina Haavio-Mannila et. al. Elmsford, N.Y.: Pergamon Press.

Sinkkonen, Sirkka, and Elina Haavio-Mannila. 1981. "The Impact of the Women's Movement and the Legislative Activity of Women's MPs on Social Development." In *Women, Power, and Political Systems,* ed. Margherita Rendel. London: Croom Helm. 195-215.

Sinkkonen, Sirkka, and Eva Hänninen. 1978. "Organizational Type, Women's Careers and Administrative and Political Involvement." Grenoble: European Consortium for Political Research.

Skard, Torild, and Elina Haavio-Mannila. 1985. "Women in Parliament." In *Unfinished Democracy: Women in Nordic Politics,* eds. Elina Haavio-Mannila et. al. Elmsford, N.Y.: Pergamon Press.

Stahlberg, Krister. 1983. "De statliga anstUallda i Finland" (Civil Service in Finland). In *Byråkrater i Norden.* (Bureaucrats in Nordic Countries), eds. Lennart Lundqvist and Krister Stalberg. Åbo: Meddelanden från Stiflelsen för Åbo Akademi Forskiningsinstitut. N. 83.

Vanhala, Sinikka. 1986. *Ekonomikunnan segmentoituneet työmarkkinat* (The Segregated Labor Market for Business Graduates). Helsinki: Helsingin kauppakorkeakoulun julkaisuja. D-81.

Vartola, Juha. 1983. *Valtionhallinnon kehittämisperiaatteista.* Tampere: Ministeriö-tutkimuksen osaraportti II. (Development Principles of State Administration. Report on the Ministries II). Tampere: Tampereen yliopisto, Julkishallinnon julkaisusarja 1.

Volanen, Risto. 1983. "Report on recruitment for the highest offices in Finland." In *Recruiting for High Offices in the Central Administration,* ed. Tor Modeen. Tampere: International Institute of Administrative Sciences, University of Tampere. Department of Administrative Sciences.

Women in Public Administration in the United States

Jane H. Bayes

BACKGROUND:
TRENDS IN THE LABOR FORCE
FOR WOMEN

The twentieth century has seen a phenomenal growth in the number of women in the paid labor force in the United States. The number doubled from 4 million or one sixth of the total labor force in 1890 to 8 million in 1910 (Lyle and Ross 1973, 2). Around 1900, the labor force participation rate for females was 19 percent. This increased to just over 25 percent by 1940, and to over 52 percent by 1985. The labor force participation rates for men declined slightly from 86.4 percent in 1950 to 55 percent in 1988 (Department of Labor 1988, 90).

The age and marital status of the woman worker has also changed. During the first decade of the century, 70 percent of female workers were single and 50 percent were under 25. Most left the work force when they were married. The median age for women workers was 26 years of age. This pattern prevailed until the post World War II period when older women began to enter the labor force in sizeable numbers to bring the median age of female workers to over 40 in the 1960s. During the 1970s and 1980s, while older women continued to work, large numbers of young women in their 20s entered the work force to bring the median age of female workers back down to 34 by 1980. Whereas in 1950 only 22 percent of all married women worked, by 1970 this percentage had jumped to 41 percent and by 1981 it was 51 percent (Department of Labor 1983, 11).

Education has also changed for women workers. In 1940, 44 percent of women had at least 4 years of high school. By 1970, over 70 percent had at least 4 years of high school, and by 1981, 83 percent had finished high school (Department of Labor 1983, 107).

Concomitant and integral to these changes in the labor force have been

85

changes in the U.S. economy. Throughout the 20th century, but particularly since World War II, the U.S. economy has been shifting from a manufacturing to a service economy. Insofar as white collar service jobs can easily be performed by women and women can be hired at lower wages than men, the demand for female labor has increased to bring older women into the labor force. Women in 1981 constitute 66 percent of the white collar labor force (Department of Labor 1983, 51).

Occupational Segregation

A major characteristic of the U.S. female labor force is the nature and stability of its sex segregation. Occupations that were 70 percent female in 1900 were largely the same occupations that were 70 percent female in 1950 and in 1980. The percentage of the female labor force in these occupations has changed with the economy. In 1900, the largest percentage of the female labor force worked as private household workers (28.7 percent). The next largest percentage was in dressmaking apparel manufacturing (12.9 percent) and 6 percent were in teaching (Oppenheimer 1970, 78-79). By 1940, women working in non-agricultural occupations were 30 percent in service occupations, 21 percent in blue collar operative jobs, and 14 percent in professional technical jobs. The service jobs were primarily waitress, hairdresser, cook, and practical nurse. Female operatives were concentrated in the apparel industry as sewing machine operators. The clerical-sales group included stenographers, typists, secretaries, bookkeepers, and retail saleswomen. Among professionals, half were teachers and another 25 percent were nurses (Waldman and McEaddy 1975).

In spite of laws enacted during the 1960s and 1970s designed to end sex discrimination and job sex segregation, occupational sex segregation continues to persist. In the 1980s, over half (55 percent) of all employed women are either in clerical (35 percent) or in service jobs (19 percent). Two of every 5 female workers were employed in only 10 occupations in 1981: secretary, bookkeeper, retail sales clerk, cashier, waitress, registered nurse, elementary school teacher, private household worker, typist, and nursing aide (Department of Labor 1983, 53). During the decade of the 1970s, women began to move in small numbers into jobs that had previously been at least 70 percent male in the past. Women made employment gains in practically all the skilled trades, in many professions such as law, medicine, accounting, pharmacy, computer science, and in some traditionally male sales occupations such as insurance, brokering, and underwriting. The fastest growing occupation for women during the decade of 1970-1980 was that of managers and administrators. Women held 18.5 percent of these jobs in 1970, 30.5 percent of them by 1980, and 39.3 percent of them in 1988.

Industrial Sex Segregation

While the occupational sex segregation of women decreased somewhat during the decade of the 1970s, the employment of women by industry continues to be profoundly segregated with change going in the direction of increased rather than decreased segregation by industry. Women dominate the finance, insurance, real estate, and service industries by two to one over men. In contrast, a much higher percentage of men are employed in mining, construction, manufacturing, transportation, and public utilities.

FEDERAL LAWS GOVERNING WOMEN'S EMPLOYMENT

The period from 1963 to 1977 was one of considerable legislative activity with regard to women. In 1938, the Fair Labor Standards Act established a minimum wage which was amended with the Equal Pay Act in 1963, and an extension of minimum wage protection to household workers in 1974. The Equal Pay Act prohibited discrimination because of sex. Title VII of the Civil Rights Act of 1964 prohibits discrimination based on sex, race, color, religion, and national origin in all terms, conditions, or privileges of employment. In 1972, this law was amended to cover all public and private employers and labor unions of 15 or more persons. The 1972 amendment also gave the bipartisan Equal Employment Opportunity Commission (EEOC), whose five members are appointed by the President, the authority to bring litigation and to extend coverage of the law.

The Federal Administrative System

The federal administrative system in the United States consists of 13 major departments having Cabinet level status, plus a large number of commissions and regulatory agencies. During World War II, federal civilian employment was at its maximum with 3.4 million persons. Since then, it has been approximately 2.8 million. Around 39 percent of these federal jobs were held by women in 1980 (Department of Labor 1983, 74). On the state level, women in 1981 constituted 42 percent of all employees, and in local government, 38 percent of local government employees were women (Department of Labor 1983, 71). Since the mid-1950s, the percentages of women in the federal civilian labor force have steadily increased from 24 percent in 1958 to almost 39 percent in 1980 (Department of Labor 1983, 74). As Table 1 shows, the concentration of women is heavily in the GS 1-8 grades (76 percent), whereas only 49 percent of all employment is in this category. In the upper grades, women constitute only 4 percent of all those in grades GS 16-18 and only 8 percent of those in the middle grades GS 13-15.

A basic hypothesis of this project was that different agencies would have different employment rates for women depending on the primary business of the agency and its relationship to traditional sex roles in the workplace. Finance has traditionally been a male occupation, whereas health and education have traditionally been female occupations. Table 2 shows the percentage of women by grade level groups for the 13 cabinet level departments in the federal government. Those having the most women in the upper grade levels are the Departments of Education (16 percent), Health and Human Services (14 percent), Housing and Urban Development (13 percent), Labor (11 percent), and State (10 percent). In the remaining departments, women constitute no more than 6% of those in the higher ranks, GS 16-18 or equivalent.

Another aspect of the federal administrative system which is important for this study is the difference between career and political appointive positions. The top ranks of the federal bureaucracy are composed of career civil servants and political appointees. The very top jobs and many near the top of the bureaucracy are political appointive offices. The rationale for this is that each President should have immediate subordinates of his own political persuasion to ensure that his policies will be administered in accordance with his overall program. Political appointees generally have different career paths from those of civil servants, although some individuals move from job to job between the two designations. A civil servant must pass competitive examinations and usually, although not always, comes at a fairly young age to work in the government as a career. Political appointees are often brought in by an Administration because of their activities and contributions to the political party of the Administration, and/or because of some expertise which they have demonstrated outside of the government, and/or because of some constituency they represent with which the Administration wants to curry favor. Once in government, they may stay as political appointees through several administrations, especially if the same political party wins the Presidency. Political appointees are more likely, however, to have their positions only during the time or part of the time one Administration is in office. As part of his attempt to control the bureaucracy, President Reagan extended his political appoint-

TABLE 1. Number and Percent of Women in Full-Time Federal White Collar Employment, by General Schedules and Equivalent Grades, October 31, 1980

General Schedule Grade	Total Employment (Men & Women)	Percent Women of Total Employment	Number of Women	Percent Distribution of All Women Employees By Grade	Women As Percent of Total Employment By Grade
Total all Pay Systems	1,985,057	100	767,117	100.	38.6
GS and Equivalent	1,472,887	100	663,962	100.	45.1
GS 1 - 8 ($7,960 - $21,875)	727,416	49	504,430	26.1	69.0
GS 9 - 12 ($18,585 - $35,033)	526,000	36	141,601	21.4	27.0
GS 13 - 15 ($32,048 - $57,912)	216,884	15	17,818	2.7	8.0
GS 16 - 18 ($52,247 - $71,734) and SES*	2,587	0.2	113	<0.05	4.0

* Senior Executive Service (SES). Civil Service Reform Act of 1978 created the SES for Grades 16 and above.

Source: U.S. Department of Labor, Women's Bureau, Time of Change: 1983 Handbook on Women Workers, Bulletin 298, 74.

TABLE 2. Percentage of Women Employed by Grade Level Grouping and by Department, 1983

DEPARTMENT	AGRICULTURE			COMMERCE			DEFENSE*		
	Number of Female Employees	Total Employees	% Female	Number of Female Employees	Total Employees	% Female	Number of Female Employees	Total Employees	% Female
GS 1 - 8	22,047	38,684	57	7,715	10,374	74	221,870	370,625	60
GS 9 - 12	5,565	39,903	14	2,526	9,804	26	53,967	223,496	24
GS 13 - 15	704	10,314	7	812	7,601	11	7,343	55,291	13
GS 16 - 18 & SES	15	340	4	28	425	6	32	1,007	3
Total	28,331	89,241	32	11,081	28,204	39	283,212	449,269	63

* These figures are for Departments of Air Force, ARmy, Defense Logistics and Navy only.

DEPARTMENT	EDUCATION			ENERGY			HEALTH & HUMAN SERVICES		
	Number of Female Employees	Total Employees	% Female	Number of Female Employees	Total Employees	% Female	Number of Female Employees	Total Employees	% Female
GS 1 - 8	1,234	1,457	92	3,708	4,695	79	50,238	59,400	85
GS 9 - 12	943	1,698	56	1,380	4,368	32	25,104	44,924	56
GS 13 - 15	424	1,482	29	625	5,600	11	3,598	16,217	22
GS 16 - 18 & SES	8	50	16	31	499	6	78	543	14
Total	2,609	4,687	56	5,745	15,162	38	79,018	121,084	65

Source: U.S. House of Representatives, Subcommittee on Employment Opportunities, Committee on Education and Labor, "The State of Affirmative Action in the Federal Government: Staff Report Analyzing 1980 and 1983 Employment Profiles," Committee Print 98th Congress 2d Session, August, 1984

DEPARTMENT

DEPARTMENT	HOUSING & URBAN DEVELOPMENT			INTERIOR			JUSTICE		
	Number of Female Employees	Total Employees	% Female	Number of Female Employees	Total Employees	% Female	Number of Female Employees	Total Employees	% Female
GS 1 - 8	3,327	3,759	89	15,222	23,163	66	8,661	14,637	59
GS 9 - 12	1,998	5,348	37	4,222	21,768	19	2,449	11,703	21
GS 13 - 15	537	2,880	19	362	3,372	11	479	2,692	18
GS 16 - 18 & SES	17	126	13	15	314	5	18	299	6
Total	5,879	12,113	49	19,821	48,617	41	11,607	29,331	40

DEPARTMENT	LABOR			STATE			TRANSPORTATION		
	Number of Female Employees	Total Employees	% Female	Number of Female Employees	Total Employees	% Female	Number of Female Employees	Total Employees	% Female
GS 1 - 8	4,786	5,626	85	1,635	2,045	80	6,778	10,119	67
GS 9 - 12	2,265	7,844	29	618	1,014	61	3,688	25,750	14
GS 13 - 15	798	4,580	17	183	630	29	821	18,480	5
GS 16 - 18 & SES	24	217	11	10	98	10	17	356	5
Total	7,873	18,267	43	2,446	3,787	65	11,304	54,705	20

DEPARTMENT	TREASURY		
	Number of Female Employees	Total Employees	% Female
GS 1 - 8	39,120	49,803	79
GS 9 - 12	12,732	38,250	33
GS 13 - 15	1,909	17,520	11
GS 16 - 18 & SES	29	518	5
Total	53,790	106,091	51

ments into many high ranking jobs that civil servants had occupied in previous administrations.

RESEARCH DESIGN AND METHODOLOGY

This study focuses on two departments in the federal government. One is concerned primarily with matters that are traditionally associated with women's occupations, the Health and Human Services Department. The other, the Treasury, deals with finance, money, and accounting, traditionally male occupational preserves. The design involved sampling the top 20 percent of the salary structure in each department and using both an interview and a written questionnaire to explore the career experiences of at least twelve women and twelve men in each department in some depth. The data for this report come from questionnaires and hour long interviews with: (1) 18 female respondents drawn by random selection from the 78 Health and Human Service employees making $59,223-$83,300 in 1985 and who also lived in Washington D.C. (Of the 94 females in this salary range within the Department, only 78 resided in Washington D.C.); and (2) 13 female respondents drawn by random selection from the 56 female Treasury Department employees in the $59,223-$83,000 salary range living in Washington D.C. in 1985. These 31 interviews with female respondents were conducted during January and February, 1985. Data for male respondents (11 from Health and Human Services and 17 from Treasury) using the same selection process and interview schedule, but a revised questionnaire form, were collected two years later in January, 1987. This paper focuses primarily on the female respondents and uses the male responses primarily as a reference to determine whether women respondents are different from men.

A Basic Description of the Sample

Table 3 presents a basic description of the sample by sex and by department. Most men and women in the positions sampled tended to be in their 40s, with very, few in their 50s and 60s. Those in high ranking positions who were in their 30s tended to be mostly women (13 out of 15) perhaps reflecting the impact of affirmative action programs. Respondents in all departments reported that affirmative action programs had had and continue to have an impact. Men and women exhibited very few differences in formal education. The individuals sampled were highly educated as a group. Over 60 percent of both sexes had post-graduate degrees. Differences between the sexes were most apparent in marriage and family statistics. Whereas 93 percent of the male sample were married, only 65 percent of the women in the sample were married. Forty-five percent of the women sampled had no children, whereas only 7 percent of the men had no children. Combining career and family continues to be more difficult for women than it is for men, although a majority of these high ranking women were married and almost half (48 percent) had children living at home at the time of the interview.

SOCIALIZATION DATA

Table 4 summarizes the socialization data obtained from the sample. Both men and women were largely the first born in their families with this being more the case for men (64 percent) than for women (46 percent). Over half of both the men and the women in the sample tended to come from families where the mother worked. The data on the highest level of education attained by either parent and the self identification of social class while growing up suggest a class difference between males and females, with women coming from families with higher education levels and higher self images in terms of class status. However, this difference is not statistically significant. What can be said is that the social class of the respondents' parents and the parents' educations showed a broad spectrum. While most respondents described their parents as middle or lower middle class, both male and female respondents had parents at both ends of the social class spectrum. One respondent had immigrant parents who had grammar school educations and worked as a waiter and a domestic. Another respondent came from a family whose parents worked as a truck driver and a garment factory worker. She came to Washington at the age of 17 with a borrowed $100 in her pocket that she repaid as soon as she had earned it. In contrast, 14 of the 59 respondents (23 percent) had at least one parent with a graduate degree and 12 of the 59 (20 percent) identified their families as being upper middle or upper class. Forty-four percent of the total sample identified their families as either lower middle or lower class.

CAREER HISTORIES
AND ASPIRATIONS

As indicated above, recruitment into the higher levels of the U.S. federal bureaucracy occurs in two distinct ways. One can be a career civil service employee or one can be a political appointee. The career histories are quite different for each although, in this sample, two women had

TABLE 3. Basic Description of Data From Respondents by Department.

	Health and Human Services	Treasury	Total
Nature of Data			
Number of Interviews	16	12	28
Number of Questionnaires	13	11	24
Age of Respondents			
30-39	6	6	12
40-49	8	5	13
50-59	1	1	2
60+	1	0	1
Total			28
Type of Appointment			
Political	8	4	12
Career	8	8	16
Total			28
Highest Degree Education			
Some College	0	1	1
College Degree	3	5	8
Masters Degree	4	4	8
Law Degree	7	2	9
PhD	2	0	2
Total			28
Marital Status			
Married	9	8	17
Single	4	3	7
Divorced, Widowed, Separated	3	1	4
Total			28
Children			
At Home	7	6	13
Yes, but not at home	2	1	3
Total with children	9	7	16
No children	7	5	12
Ethnic Identity			
Yes, Jewish	2	0	2
Yes, Black	2	1	3
Yes, Swedish	1	0	1
No	8	9	17
Not Available	3	2	5

Religion
Protestant	5	5	10
Catholic	2	4	6
Jewish	2	0	2
None	4	1	5
Not Available	3	2	5

Political Party
Republicans	9	3	12
Democrats	5	5	10
Independent	2	4	6

Grade Level or Rank
GS 15	1	4	5
SES	15	8	23

switched during their careers. Some women with political appointments began their careers either by working in political campaigns and/or by working for a congressman or senator. These individuals, once they have obtained a bureaucratic appointment, may maintain and use their Congressional political networks. Other women with political appointments have been recruited to perform in an area in which they have special expertise. They may or may not have been active in local politics. Still others are brought into an Administration with a political appointment as a political reward or because of the local or special constituency that the individual brings with her. Career civil servants tend to fall into one of two categories: those who have worked their way up in the same agency doing a variety of different tasks and those who have moved around from department to department and who make a practice of moving laterally and then being promoted once they are in a new job. Men and women tend to differ in their career history patterns. Men in top positions in our sample were more likely to have advanced within their agencies by a margin of 61 percent to 25 percent. The women were divided almost equally between those in civil service careers and those who had obtained their high position by political appointment. Both men and women in about equal proportions (32 percent and 29 percent) advanced by moving from one department to another in their careers.

Career Aspirations

The career aspirations for the sample were somewhat varied with no particular differences between men and women. Several noted that the "top is filled." Twelve respondents indicated that they would like to

TABLE 4. Summary of Socialization

Childhood Role Model		Adult Mentors		Highest Level of Education Attained by Either Parent		Social Class	
Mother	6	Female Lawyer	1	Graduate Degree	8	Upper	1
Father	2	No one Person	2	BA or BS	4	Upper Middle	6
Parents	4	Male Professor	2	Some College	5	Middle	7
Mother or Friend	1	Male Boss	6	High School	5	Lower Middle	6
Peer	1	Husband and Others	2	Elementary School	2	Working	4
Mother and Aunt	1	Male Superiors	1	Not Available	4	Not Available	4
None	4	Female Colleagues	3				
Not Available	6	None	2				
Good at School	2	Not Available	1				
School Principal	1						

Working Status of Parents		Birth Order	
Both Worked	16	1st or Only	13
Father Worked	8	2nd	5
Not Available	4	3rd	1
		4th	1
		Not Available	8

"move up" in the organization or obtain a Presidential appointment. One woman noted that she found it most rewarding to move laterally to keep herself challenged by her work. Ten respondents expressed a desire to move into private industry in the future. Eleven others (eight men, three women) indicated that they were happy where they were. One expressed a desire to move into some World Health organization or to go into higher education administration. About five individuals had worked in the private sector prior to coming to government or they had taken time out of their government careers to work in industry for a year.

THE JOB SITUATION

A number of general trends emerged from the data which explored the job situation of each respondent in some depth. First, consider work hours. All the female respondents spend at least 9 hours a day at work. All but one of the four women who reported staying at work no more than 45 hours a week were women with young or teenage children. In contrast, almost half of the males in the sample reported spending between 41 and 50 hours a week at work. Several of the mothers discussed the tradeoffs they had to make in this area. One woman wished that her family life would allow her to be at work early—before others. Another noted that family life prevented her from mixing socially and professionally as much as she would like. Most of the women reported working through the lunch hour every day or several times during the week. About a third of both the women and the men reported that they regularly work 10 to 12 hours a day. Others noted that when Congress is in session, their hours increase. Several of the men reported spending more than sixty hours a week at the job. Three women expressed the view that they had a personal policy about being a workaholic, that it was bad management to work too much, and expressed the opinion that the agency tended to reward workaholics and that there was a kind of macho ethic concerning who worked harder than who. Two of these same women reported that they regularly work a 10 hour day. One woman said that she used to be a workaholic in that she did nothing but work to the point that she sometimes spent the night at the office. However, in the last year and a half, she has made a conscious decision to stop working so much. She reported that it really has not made a difference in the performance of her job. Several women noted that they worked harder than their colleagues or even than their superiors. Others commented that the top management put in very long hours.

The Job Responsibilities for Women

The range of duties and responsibilities which respondents have is impressive and diverse. Four female respondents were managers or supervisors of programs involving from 260 to 5000 employees. Others supervised staffs of between 4 and 35 involved in specific research, legal counsel, or other specialized areas of expertise. Two were responsible for a central office in Washington and for regional offices in the field. The sample contained six Assistant Secretaries or Deputy Assistant Secretaries. These women either reported directly to the Secretary of the Department or had only one person between themselves and the Secretary. (A Secretary of a Department has Cabinet rank.) Five members of the sample were lawyers working as Associate, Assistant, and Deputy Assistant General Counsel. Two respondents were close Executive or Press Secretaries either to a Secretary or an Assistant Secretary. Nine Directors of agencies that generally reported to an Assistant Secretary or a Deputy Assistant Secretary were a part of the sample. These agencies all had specialized functions requiring special expertise. Two Commissioners or Assistant Commissioners, a Program Manager and two Deputy Directors constituted the remainder of the female sample. As noted above, women are by no means as numerous in the top levels of the federal bureaucracy, but at least some of them hold important positions.

What the Female Respondents Like About Their Work

The most predominant single response to this question concerned the satisfaction these women experienced in being able to influence public policy at a high level. Eleven of the respondents mentioned this. Others mentioned that they enjoyed the freedom and autonomy "to target work efforts and resources" or to control their own work schedule and choose the issues on which they would work. Many mentioned that they enjoyed the challenge and variety of their jobs. The prestige of the job, the contact with "high level officials and hot issues" and the fact that "people pay attention to what I say" were all mentioned. Finally, many women explained that they enjoyed the content or subject matter of the job: being involved with specific areas of public policy, legislative drafting, legal work, supervising functions, getting money back for the government, "the operational environment requiring fast thinking and timely decisions," and "being forced to learn technologies that I have avoided in the past."

What Female Respondents Disliked About Their Jobs

Most of the respondents were satisfied with their jobs. On a scale of 1 to 5, nine respondents rated their satisfaction as very high (a #1 rating); twelve respondents checked #2 on the scale. The remaining three respondents who answered this question checked #s 3, 4, and 5 on the scale respectively indicating the degree of their dissatisfaction. The respondents' comments concerning what they disliked about their jobs varied considerably. Pressure, fatigue, stress, "having to please so many egos," and "the exhausting pace" were common responses. Frustration at the slowness of the bureaucracy and frustration with the "obstructive nature of the political environment (or Congress) which often undermines important programs," "political pressure gets in the way of substance," "game playing by top male managers who subordinate programs to ego massaging and power trips" were mentioned. Other respondents mentioned "dealing with problem performers," "confrontation with employees," and "being in the role of critic, problem finder" as unpleasant aspects of their jobs. Two mentioned that they did not like the subject matter of their jobs. Another group of responses concerned not having enough authority or power, "not enough influence over agency decision," "poor power position," "being made to feel I am intruding on the authority of my supervisor," "my speciality is not considered important."

Special Skills of the Female Respondents

When asked what they were good at doing, the respondents agreed on a number of general skills such as writing, thinking clearly, communicating, speaking, negotiating, managing, organizing, and mediating. Many mentioned that they were good at conceptualizing and problem solving. Others emphasized their interpersonal skills. Finally, respondents mentioned that their specialized knowledge was important, whether it be of the law, of particular areas of legislation, of Congress, of grants, or of personnel matters.

Management Style of the Respondents

A number of women spoke of their style as being straight and to the point.

I have been characterized as being strong, direct, curt, and short. I just think that I am being frank and not wasting a lot of time socializing . . .

I am not very diplomatic. I have never developed the talent for diplomacy. I have a godawful frankness with enough humor to take the awful edge off frankness, and sometimes not, intentionally.

Another group spoke of achieving some kind of balance.

I attempt to be an iron hand in a velvet glove. I try to be firm and forceful but also try to be very ladylike and diplomatic. I try to meld the macho maleness . . . not the macho maleness but the stubbornness and bullishness that the man has with a style that is not offensive and yet try not to be dictatorial. I try to be open and listen and yet, when I make a decision, I try to be decisive.

I smile all the time, but I write nasty memos.

I am not afraid to fire people who do not perform and to take disciplinary action when people don't do what they are supposed to. On the other hand, I am glad to reward those who perform very well and recognize and appreciate people who put in the extra effort.

One set of responses emphasized teamwork and cooperation.

I work very hard to get subordinates that report to me to work together as a collegial team. I consult with them on everything. My predecessor had a one-on-one style. I try to build a board of directors and build on that.

I get people to trust me because I don't have hidden agendas. I am not formal, so I invite lots of comment and input. I followup. But when I think that everyone is marching in step, I try to cut them loose. I then support the hell out of them. I have gone on the mat for money, funding, giving people exposure that they have never had before. People like that. They like being trusted.

Another style mentioned by several women involved interpersonal skills.

I get along with people well. I am not intimidated and not intimidating. I am good at analyzing and problem solving and finding a way to do it. I am very collegial. I toss out ideas and have others give them back in different form. I delegate a lot and try not to interfere too much with the mechanisms by which the results are obtained. It works very well with a professional staff.

I talk about different styles a lot with one of my friends. His style when he has something to sell is to put together a slick presentation to dominate the audience and to convince everyone with his presentation. He wins every time. He is brilliant. I don't compete with him. I take someone for lunch. I go up to talk with my boss in the afternoon. I catch people in the ladies' room. A lot of the power around here is female.

A final group of responses to the inquiry about personal style mentioned concern with control.

I like to manage by objectives. I really believe in accountability . . . I am very clear with my staff about outcome. They know that I am very concerned about accountability. I set a real model for them. I don't let a memo go forward that I personally have not read. When I sign off, I've read it . . .

I am reasonably good at coordinating and controlling and getting out quality pieces of work and keeping tabs on the work . . . My subordinates get recognized. I push them hard and they get recognized with awards and honors.

In comparing the management styles of women with those of men, the data suggest that while some women are particularly concerned with interpersonal skills, in some agencies, men are too. The "culture" of the agency may have more to do with predominant management styles in that agency than do any inherent distinctions between men and women with regard to management style.

Networks, Support Systems and Social Life at the Office

Many of the women in the sample reported a certain loneliness that accompanied their jobs.

Being a woman, it can be lonely at the top. There are some conventions about the degree to socialize and there are so few associates who are at peer level. I am outgoing, but not a social calendar person. Unless there is a particular work urgency, I have some difficulty calling a man and asking him for lunch. I find it difficult to ask someone for lunch just for company. Part of it is working with people who are generally older. They are just not altogether comfortable.

It is a very lonesome place. I would be the first to admit that if you want to let your hair down, you do it with old friends, because with your professional counterparts, you never know. Is she getting ready to leave? Where is she going to go? Washington is one of those kind of places. It is true for men, too, I am sure. The higher you get, this is a very hard and cold place. Men have different kinds of networks. Men have fraternity networks and they come in from industry and go back. They have that kind of revolving door and that kind of network. This is especially true for political appointments. It is not true for women. Women are not in fields that have that kind of revolving door situation . . . Women haven't developed that. Maybe in another generation . . .

I don't have a network. I wish I did. I feel isolated.

Some women recognize that some of the isolation is of their own making.

I need to work more on pushing myself socially.

My boss is a really nice guy. He respects me and his boss is really nice. Once they asked me to go out to lunch with them. They go out once a week. I said no. But if I wanted to go out to lunch with them there would be no problem at all. It is because they know that I don't go out to lunch.

We had a planning conference last year. The way the tables were set up to eat dinner they were six, four, and two. My boss and I sat at a table for two. It was the first time we had ever eaten together. He tried to explain that it doesn't mean anything. I know that part of it is me, but that is why there is no network. But I don't feel the need for it either.

Socialize? Not here. This is a male dominated agency. I have no interest in socializing here.

I don't do much socializing. Even when I am invited to receptions, I don't go. I am burned out on receptions.

Still other respondents, all in the Health and Human Services Department, reported that in their particular agencies there was a very friendly climate, at least on the surface. They reported that everyone went out to lunch with everyone else. One group had a practice of drinking beer on Friday afternoons after work. One group even went on frequent weekend outings together.

When asked about networks of friends who served as supporters and advisors, most of the respondents indicated that they did not have networks, or they mentioned certain groups such as Executive Women in Government that passes around job information, or the Treasury Women's Network that sponsors seminars and workshops for women. The Health and Human Services Department did not have a departmental women's network. Other respondents reported that they kept in touch with colleagues from past jobs, with people on the Hill, with personnel people, with organizations concerned with specific policies and legislation, with colleagues in higher education or in the private sector, or with old political friends outside of Washington. Many of those who had neither a network nor did much socializing did report having a relationship with one or several close professional male and/or female friends, often outside of their own agency, with whom they had lunch frequently and "talked shop" and/or discussed careers.

CHILDREN AND FAMILY LIFE

Thirteen of the 28 women in the sample had children living at home. The methods of coping were varied; however, one woman expressed a common theme when asked how it was to raise a family and work in her position.

> It is hard and anyone who tells you it isn't must either have $8 billion dollars and be able to hire everybody or else they are lying. You get up at least two hours earlier than your friends. You do everything ahead of time because you never know. You pray that you don't ever get sick because you can't afford to. The biggest issue that every woman who has children has is childcare. Who is going to be there to provide the quality childcare that we are committed to? The resolution of that became the major factor in every job I have had. That had to be taken care of first before I could go out the door. When I did go out the door, I would block it out of my mind. It's the only way to survive. And then when you go home, it is a whole refocus. And that is basically what you do because you have to. I am an unbelievable listmaker. I have lists here, I have lists at home. I have lists stuck on the bulletin board. . . . It is tough sledding. It is just unbelievable what you do.

As noted above, most of the women with children do not work quite as long hours at the office as those who do not have children, although they all report being at the office for over 9 hours each day. The arrangements for childcare in the morning and in the evening and for other activities differ. Husbands also take various degrees of responsibility for child raising among the couples in the sample. Two of the respondents are single parents. Five of the 13 with children at home report that their husbands love the children, that they play with them, and they will do things for the children when asked, but that they do not take responsibility for them in the sense of making sure that they get their shots, that they are fed, clothed, and schooled properly, and that they get to and from their activities. Three of the thirteen reported a shared parenting situation. These couples stagger their work hours and divide and share duties and responsibilities. In one situation, the husband was responsible for all housekeeping and child rearing activities. Those women who are single parents with young children have live-in help arrangements. This was also true for many of the women when their children were of preschool age.

The five married women in the sample who bear primary responsibility for their children hire help for after school or they depend on other mothers to help with carpooling their children to various activities. They then work hard at finding ways of reciprocating which will not interfere with their work schedule. It is these women who reported most vociferously their feelings of guilt or of being torn in two directions. Two women spoke of feeling guilty later.

> I know that my daughter has experienced periods of loneliness. Should I have paid more attention? She's in high school now. She has lots of friends and a very active social life. Yesterday, I asked her if she liked tapioca. She said yes. I said, 'Well you know what, Pam, I am going to make you tapioca someday.' My mother was always making things like tapioca. — I feel that I have shortchanged myself not having the flexibility to do all the carpooling and so forth. I feel torn.

Factors Which Have Helped Women's Advancement the Most

When asked to identify the factors that helped the women's movement, the respondents mentioned affirmative action and equal opportunity laws most often. Other external factors mentioned included the economy, fertility control, more labor force participation by women, and the scarcity of enough qualified persons to fill management jobs. Leadership from the top was often mentioned. In addition to factors external to women, many cited the activities and achievements of women themselves. The publicized success of the first women to break sex barriers and serve as role models was mentioned by several of them. Increased knowledge, increased education, and increased experience at high levels of management along with hard work, perseverance, and determination were mentioned by many respondents. Some of the factors considered by some as advancing women are considered by others as a barrier. For example, some women identify overaggressiveness as being a barrier to women. Others suggest that lack of aggressiveness is a major problem. Some women think affirmative action programs have been extremely important to the advancement of women; others think that they encourage the appointment of incompetent women who then damage the advancement of other more capable women.

Attitudes Towards Feminism

At the very end of the interview, the interviewer asked each respondent to define what the word "feminism" meant to her. The following question was: Are you a feminist? This question elicited some very interesting and often somewhat contradictory opinions from the respondents. Of the 22 respondents replying to this inquiry, only 5 said that they were feminists, and even some of these placed qualifications on their identification. All but one of these respondents were in the Department of Health and Human Services. All the remaining women respondents were either unwilling to call themselves feminists or else were careful to dissociate themselves with feminism unless the concept were carefully defined as equal opportunity and equal treatment for women and not some radical bra burning activity. Many of these women had described incidents of discrimination in their own lives. Many had consciously made an effort to help other women.

One woman in the Treasury Department may have explained this reluctance for most of these women to call themselves feminists. She said, "I think that if I were very active in the women's movement, I wouldn't have gotten where I am now. I can also say that I wouldn't stay here." Most of the respondents fell into the category of associating feminism with bra burning, aggressive, man-hating activism, or else with the concept of advocacy for women. They denied that they were feminists, but then they went on to say that they believed in equal opportunity for women and that women should have the opportunity to work or not to work in the paid labor force. At least some of the responses to these questions reflected a sophisticated understanding of the contributions of what they called "the bra burners," even though they wanted to distance themselves from any activity of that sort and were unwilling to call themselves feminists except in the sense that feminism meant equal opportunity and equal treatment for women.

OTHER GENERAL FINDINGS:
SEXUAL HARASSMENT

All of the respondents indicated that sexual harassment was not a problem for them at their level. One woman had experienced sexual harassment in a government agency in the sense of being hounded to go out by a male superior when she was younger. She reported running down the halls and hiding in the ladies' room to avoid this man. Another respondent reported that the man she replaced had left because of numerous reports of sexual harassment by his subordinates. Other women said that they had heard of cases of sexual harassment in their past experience, especially those who had worked in the private sector, but did not regard it as a major problem at present in their agency.

Discrimination

Many of the women, sometimes without being specifically asked, gave examples of incidents of discrimination that had occurred in their careers. One black woman said that over the years she had experienced more discrimination from being female than she had from being black. Two women spoke of being told that they could not have an expected promotion because they would then make more than their husbands. A number of lawyers and one accountant said that they joined the government as young professionals because the private sector would not hire them. Even today, several respondents indicated that the female applicants with law degrees have much higher qualifications than the male applicants. Respondents spoke of the "old boy network" which exists at both the Treasury Department and at the Health and Human Services Department below the Secretarial level. (The Secretary is a woman.) One respondent said that this network was particularly effective in distributing merit awards and bonuses to members of the network.

A number of women gave examples of difficulty in first entering the work force with an advanced degree and constantly being asked in the job interview whether they could type. One respondent when the question came again during an interview said, "No, can you?" She did not get the job. Another said she took a job at Bank of America because it was the first job interview she had had in four months that didn't ask her how fast she could type. She had a masters degree in journalism. She also reported that there was much less discrimination in Washington. "There is much better acceptance of women working than there is in other cities."

OVERALL CONCLUSIONS:
GENERAL STRATEGIES FOR IMPROVEMENT

While it may seem difficult to generalize from a sample of 28 respondents, the universe from which they are drawn, women residing in Washington who are GS 15 or above in the Health and Human Services Department and the Treasury Department, is small, consisting of 128 individuals. If all the women at GS 15 and above living outside of Washington were added it would increase the pool by only 30 persons. For men, the universe is much larger since the combined upper ranks of the Health and Human Services and Treasury Departments are only about 10 percent female.

A clear difference in culture existed between the Health and Human Services Department and the Treasury Department especially with regard to the situation of women. Women in the Treasury Department express many more feelings of constraint with regard to their female identity. In this agency with the few women at the top, it is more dangerous politically to identify with female causes. Women in the Treasury Department seem to have more at stake in assuring themselves and others of their professionalism, their competence, their worthiness to be in the position that they are in regardless of their sex. In the Health and Human Services Department, respondents were more comfortable identifying themselves with feminist causes. Even among those who do consider themselves feminists, the understanding of feminism is primarily in terms of equal opportunity. While a few women (4) expressed an appreciation for the "bra-burners" in an historical sense, none of the women (except perhaps one indirectly) seemed to know about or understand the concepts and objectives of radical feminism as a political movement. One woman made it very clear that a rejection of active feminism was clearly a strategy that women must adopt if they are to survive in high positions in the federal government. This does not mean that these women do not work to promote women and women's issues. Several are in a position to influence major legislation with regard to women and have made major contributions in bettering the lives of women through such actions as making credit laws and regulations more equitable for women or in pointing out to Congress how certain proposed pieces of legislation hurt women such as provision to the Aid For Dependent Children program not to pay benefits unless they were over $10, which would in turn eliminate eligibility for state medicare programs in many states. This would affect many women and their children. In this latter case, the respondent gave the example to illustrate her ability to think through the consequences of proposed legislation. She did not use the example to illustrate her commitment to women. As a civil servant, she is not supposed to be an advocate. She herself was one who had hostile feelings about feminism.

The degree of consciousness about helping other women seemed to vary roughly in relation to the respondent's identification as a feminist. Many indicated that they tried to help both men and women subordinates with their careers. Those who identified as feminists cited several examples of talented women they had "found," promoted, and often encouraged to move on to further their careers.

Strategies with regard to networking were not central to the consciousness of the respondents. Many indicated that they were slightly involved with the Treasury Women's Network or with Executive Women in Government or with various professional groups both inside and outside of Washington. All the respondents reported close personal relationships with both men and women that they used as support systems for advice and as sounding boards for ideas and possible future strategies. Usually these groups were small and, for over half, they were at least partially if not entirely male in composition.

The career histories of the women indicated a marked difference for political and career appointments, as discussed above. Among the careerists, about half had worked their way up in the same agency, while the other half had developed strategies of moving laterally and then getting promoted. The political appointees also varied. All but one of the political appointees had come to Washington with the Reagan Administration. Some had had varied careers in political campaign organizations, working as staff in state governments, and/or working as staff for members of Congress. Others were recruited from the private sector, from industry, and from education because of their expertise and, in some cases, because of their political participation. Some of the political appointees were moving out of government and back into industry now "before the rush" at the end of the Reagan administration in 1988. Others spoke of plans to move within the next two years for the same reason. The fact that the Administration was Republican in 1985-87 when this study was conducted influenced this study tremendously in that the backgrounds and attitudes of the female political appointees in a Democratic Administration probably would be quite different. Twelve of the 28 respondents were political appointments.

Perhaps the most common theme that emerged in considering the possibilities for advancement of career women in the future related to the small number of positions at the top, the relatively young age of most of the women who have broken into the top ranks, and the small number of retirements and/or openings that are likely to be available to either women or men for the next 20 years. This observation, of course, assumes that the percentages of women in the top political appointee ranks of the federal government departments will remain at their current low levels. Given the present political era in the United States, that assumption is not unrealistic.

REFERENCES

Lyle, Jerolyn R., and Jane L. Ross. 1973. *Women in Industry: Employment Patterns in Corporate America*. Lexington, Mass: D.C. Heath.

Oppenheimer, Valerie Kincade. 1970. *The Female Labor Force in the United States: Demographic and Economic Factors Governing Its Growth and Changing Composition, Population Monograph Series No 5*. University of California, Berkeley: Institute of International Studies.

U.S. Department of Labor, Bureau of Labor Statistics. 1988. *Handbook of Labor Statistics*. Washington, DC: U.S. Government Printing Office.

U.S. Department of Labor Women's Bureau. 1983. *Time of Change: 1983 Handbook on Women Workers*, Bulletin 298

U.S. House of Representatives. 1984. Subcommittee on Employment Opportunities, Committee on Education and Labor, "The State of Affirmative Action in the Federal Government: Staff Report Analyzing 1980 and 1983 Employment Profiles," Committee Print. 98th Congress, 2d Session, August, 1984.

Waldman, Elizabeth, and Beverly J. McEaddy. 1975. "Where Women Work— An Analysis by Industry and Occupations," U.S. Department of Labor, Bureau of Labor Statistics, Bulletin 1868.

Women and Public Administration: A Comparative Perspective — Conclusion

Jane H. Bayes

The initial aim of this research effort was to assess the status of women in top administrative positions and to document and compare the prevalence of various barriers to women's advancement in public administration in several countries. The expectation was that women in public administration would have similar experiences cross-nationally. The question was, how similar would these barriers be and where would the differences lie? Studies of the status of women in a variety of countries throughout the world during the Women's Decade make it clear that the differences between women of different cultures, histories, and economic circumstances are substantial despite the similarities of childbearing, child rearing, and general economic, social, and political subordination to men that characterize women in all cultures (Morgan 1984; Seager and Olson 1986; Lovenduski 1986; Iglitzin and Ross 1986). Of the variables involving difference, religion and economic organization may have the largest impact on the socialization of women and on women's access to education. The organization of the state also is significant as states assume different functions in socialist, developing, and advanced capitalist economies as well as in democracies of various types, military dictatorships, and communist regimes. Federal versus central bureaucratic organization may also be important.

PROBLEMS OF COMPARISON

As noted in the Introduction, the data collected for this study indicate that the ways different societies treat women and women in top administrative positions are similar in some aspects and, at the same time, also quite unique to each individual society. What seem to be quite similar outcomes may be defined by very, different conditions. The intellectual dilemma is not unlike the struggle many Western feminists have been having with the concept of the patriarchy. The patriarchy is useful as a concept because it unites women in showing that women's oppression is universal and global. At the same time, the concept in itself may be oppressive to women in that it obscures very real and important differences among women. Perhaps the most that can be done in a comparison of this nature is to note the similarities at the same time as one notes the differences. This symposium conclusion, first, will compare the data for the various countries according to the questions posed by the common research interview and questionnaire instruments. A summary of the distinguishing characteristics of the findings for each country will follow. Finally, to give context to the comparative enterprise, a discussion of some of the major differences between the countries and the position of women within them will set the stage for the argument that the similarities that describe women in top administrative positions and the barriers they continue to experience in all the countries of this symposium are not easily correlated with other variables measured in this study. The evidence does support the importance of the structure of the economy, the role of the state in the economy and in the society, and the structure of the labor force in establishing the possibilities for women in higher administrative positions. Access to appropriate higher education for women is another critical variable supported by the findings of this study. Yet these factors alone do little to explain some of the important similarities or differences in socialization and experience that the respondents reported.

A Comparison of Interview and Questionnaire Data: Numbers of Women in Top Positions

A comparison of the interview and questionnaire data gathered in each country generates a number of observations. First, women are in top positions in the public bureaucracies of all of these countries. However, their numbers are limited. Comparison is difficult because it is not clear where the line between "top" and "upper level" or "middle level" should be drawn in any country. The research group decided to define the top 10 percent of the salary structure as "top level" for purposes of comparative sampling. In practice, the small number of women in "top" administrative jobs in several countries meant that researchers had to expand the definition of "top level" to include women in "upper level" and even "middle level" in some cases. The Bulgarian data are particularly difficult as the government makes no distinction between public and private enterprises. Ananieva and Razvigorova report that women constituted 30 percent of all managerial positions in Bulgaria in 1984; however, their data do not identify how many of these women are in the top ranks of the managerial cadre. In spite of these difficulties, some comparisons are possible. In the Netherlands, women compose 2 and 5 percent of the top two salary levels. In the United States, women constituted 7 percent of the top administrative levels (GS 16-18 and the Senior Executive Service, SES) as a whole in 1983. In the Agriculture, Defense, and Treasury Departments women were in fewer than 6 percent of the top jobs and in Departments like Health and Human Services and Education they held as many as 16 percent of the top positions. Langkau-Herrmann and Sessar-Karpp report that in Germany, less than 1 percent of the top grade of the civil service are women, and only 6 percent of the upper grade civil service are women. Only 17 percent of the full-time civil service employees were women. The report from Finland indicates that while women have made significant inroads in obtaining top positions in parliament and in party politics, only one or two women hold positions in the top levels of the bureaucracy. In the middle levels of the bureaucracy, women constitute 13 percent of the assistant department heads (4th highest level in the hierarchy) and 9 percent of all bureau heads. In India, the elite Indian Administrative Services has no more than 11 percent women.

EDUCATION AND SOCIAL BACKGROUND

All the women in the top levels of the administration in each country exhibited high levels of education. In most countries, a university degree or performance on a competitive examination is a minimum qualification for entry into the civil service ranks. The United States sample included a number of women who had entered the civil service at a lower level without a degree. In most cases, these women acquired a degree at a later date.

The social background of top women administrators varies considerably according to country. In India, the top female administrators in the sample all came from fairly well-educated families. Forty-five percent of the sample were upper caste Hindu women. Thirty-one percent of the sample had fathers who were in the public service. Over 40 percent of the sample came from an upper income level group. While the United States sample had representatives of all social class backgrounds, Bulgaria exhibited perhaps the greatest social mobility. Only one woman in the sample of 20 top female administrators had a parent with more than a secondary level education.

FAMILY, MARRIAGE, AND CHILDREN

In all of the countries considered here, the percentage of the top women sampled in each country who were married varied rather drastically. In Bulgaria, 85 percent were married; in India, 74 percent; in the United States, 60 percent (90 percent of the men in top positions were married); in Finland, 56 percent; in Germany, 42 percent (78 percent of the men in the top grade were married); in the Netherlands, only 16 percent of the women in the sample were married although 50 percent of the sample was either married or cohabiting. The number of children also varied. In Finland and in the United States, top male managers tended to have more children than top female managers. In both the Finnish and the United States samples, 45 percent of the women administrators had no children. In the United States, only 4 percent of the sample of males did not have any children. In Germany, 25 percent of the sample of women had children. In the Netherlands, only 16 percent of the sample had children, although other women in the sample were young enough to contemplate the prospect. In Bulgaria, all the married women had children. In India, the women in the sample had much smaller families than is the average for India. The average number of children for the women in the I.A.S. sample was one, while the average number of children per woman for all of India in 1981 was over five.

AGE

Indian women were not allowed to enter the prestigious Indian Administrative Services until 1951, which helps to explain why 90 percent of the Indian sample were under 45 years old. In the Netherlands, 75 percent of the interviewed women were between 32 and 40 years of age. In Finland, with its longer tradition of having women involved in the labor force, 72 percent of the sample of top administrators were 40 years of age and older. The same age structure characterizes the women in the German and Bulgarian samples where 87 percent and 85 percent respectively were over 40 years old. In the United States, the highest proportion (48 percent) of the women in the sample of top administrators were between 40-49 years of age. For the male sample, 74 percent were between 40-49. Forty-one percent of the female sample were between 30-39 in age while only 7 percent of the males in comparable positions were in this younger age bracket. Perhaps in response to affirmative action policies and in the absence of older women in career ladder chains, women have recently been able to move into top positions at younger ages than men in the United States.

BARRIERS TO ADVANCEMENT

When asked to identify the factors that were barriers to women's advancement, women in every country tended to list some factors characteristic of the society as a whole; some factors characteristic of public administration structures and practices; and some factors peculiar to women themselves. Among the social contextual factors were the general perception of the society as a whole that women are inferior, the lack of child care programs, the lack of education and training for women, and the lack of family support. Factors that relate to the public bureaucracies themselves include: unwillingness to be flexible enough to accommodate women trying to raise children; recruitment and promotion practices that discriminate against women; masculine traditions and networks; lack of positive female role models; and unwillingness of men to give women "good" positions or assignments that could help the women advance. Factors that are peculiar to women themselves include such items as lack of self-confidence, lack of ambition, commitment to family responsibilities over job responsibilities; lack of experience, education, ability, and/or hard work; failure by women to plan and monitor their careers; and unwillingness to take risks. Factors that women administrators agree have facilitated the advancement of women include: the growing proportion of women in the public sector; leadership from the top; legal changes; the growing competence, training, education, and experience of women; the development of women's networks; the growing global women's movement; the increased participation of women in political activities of all sorts; and the scarcity of well-qualified persons for management jobs.

MANAGEMENT STYLE

Many of the female respondents in all countries reported their managerial style to be more "open," more "democratic," more "consensual," or more "participatory" than the management styles of men. The West German study found women to engage in more democratic, consultative styles of management. In the United States study the data supported the hypothesis that women have democratic, consultative management styles, however the data show that at least some men also use democratic, consultative styles. The style of management in an organization may depend more on the "culture" of the organization than on the gender of the administrators. The United States data do suggest that the percentage of women in the top levels of an organization affects the behavior of women in that organization. As organizations begin to approach having women in 20 percent of their top leadership positions, the environment for women changes. When top women are few in number, they must adopt male behavior patterns in many instances to survive. In contrast, when women constitute over 20 percent of an organization, they can begin to identify and act as women with less chance of retribution. They can even begin to network and do some organizing. In the top levels of every country's bureaucracy, the percentage of women in the top echelons is considerably less than 20 percent, although in the United States women occupy between 13 and 16 percent of the top positions in some departments like Education and Health and Human Services. The interview data in the United States showed very different attitudes about dress, about speech, and about political activity for women among those respondents in the agency with the larger proportion of women in top positions.

SOME UNIQUE CHARACTERISTICS
OF EACH COUNTRY AS A WHOLE

The status of women in public administration in each of the six studies reflects conditions and priorities peculiar to the history and culture of each country. India is special in that it is a large nation hovering between modernity and tradition. Both the Hindu and Muslim religions play a large role in the society. Women constitute only 25 percent of the waged labor force in India, and almost 50 percent of the female labor force works as agricultural laborers. Eighty percent of the population is rural. Because of these characteristics, the barriers for women administrators in India are similar to those in many of the traditional agricultural societies of Asia, Africa, and Latin America. In 1981, only 25 percent of the Indian female population were literate compared to 47 percent of the male population. Traditional social norms which define marriage as the main vocation for women continue to be widespread and powerful. At the same time, more women are becoming educated. Women's employment in the service sector and especially in the public service has been increasing. In 1977, women constituted 52 percent of all employees in the public sector. The inheritance of the British Civil Service during the colonial period is very apparent in the recruitment procedures and requirements of the civil service where a graduate degree is a minimum qualification for entry. Swarup and Sinha in their interviews discovered that most of the women in the top administrative positions of the civil service were well-educated themselves and from well-educated families with relatively high incomes. Many of the women (31 percent) had fathers who were or had been in the civil service. In a variety of other ways, such as late marriage, love marriage, urban background, and small family size, the women in the Indian sample exhibit the characteristics of a modernized elite group operating in a society that maintains largely traditional cultural traditions and norms. The top women administrators must cope with this disjunction in the conflicting everyday social pressures that develop between their roles at home and their roles in the office. While this phenomenon exists for women in all countries, the gap between the modern world of public administration inspired by the British and the traditional world of most Indian women is much greater than it is in any European country or in the United States.

Bulgaria represents the category of countries having a state directed economy where the Communist ideology, a government committed to modernization, and a shortage of labor, especially educated labor, have encouraged the state to declare women the equal of men, to educate women, and to integrate women into practically all occupations in the economy.

Bulgaria is unique in that its women have had a history of political involvement while resisting Ottoman and Nazi oppression. In a country that emerged from World War II as a traditional agricultural society where most of the population, particularly women, did not have higher education, Bulgarian women have made enormous strides in the last few decades. The socialist revolution of 1944 with its emphasis on social and economic development has meant that women have been recruited into education and into production in traditionally male fields such as law, engineering, and economics in a way that has not occurred to the same degree in non-socialist countries. While traditional patterns of sex segregation persist in that women continue to be primarily responsible for homemaking and child care, state policies encourage women to participate in the labor force by providing child care and other social services. Although the state is pushing both men and women to accept new egalitarian roles for women, Ananieva and Razvigorova report that almost half of the women in their sample were reluctant to accept high administrative posts and were somewhat dissatisfied with their jobs. Only about a third of the sample expressed an enthusiasm for administrative work. Many of the women in the Bulgarian sample were more interested in working in their specialties rather than as "functionaries" or managers. The rewards of more responsibility and somewhat higher pay in a society where consumer goods are scarce are not particularly attractive to many women in Bulgaria. This lack of desire among women for higher positions reported by Ananieva and Razvigorova could be due to a number of other factors as well, such as the lack of prestige given top administrative positions open to women; state or party influence in directing career choices for the administrators; and the socialization of women, a frustrating bureaucracy, or the increased difficulty of combining family responsibilities with a time consuming responsible position in a society where daily living is difficult.

The status of women in the industrialized nations of the United States and Western Europe is differentiated from the status of women in state driven industrializing countries and in more traditional or colonial agricultural societies in that the pressure for women to break traditional barriers comes not so much from the top down but rather more from grassroot pressures spurred by the economy and trends in the labor market as well as by women's political activities.

In the Netherlands, historical conditions have operated to keep women out of the work force in a way that is unique in comparison with other European countries. While women constitute around 50 percent of the work force in other European countries (with the exception of Germany and Ireland) in the 1980s, in the Netherlands only 35 percent of the employed were women. Whereas 39 percent of all women were in the paid labor force, only 18 percent of married women were in the paid labor force. Socialization patterns which Leyenaar describes as "the culture of motherhood" are reflected in the fact that in 1981 only 16 percent of those women under 35 with small children were employed as compared with 75 percent of those in the same age group without children. This pattern of career interruption is extremely important in explaining why more women are not in the top echelons of the bureaucracy in the Netherlands. The widespread "culture of motherhood" has serious implications for the recruitment into the bureaucracy of talented young women. Many believe they must choose between career and family.

The situation in Germany as reported by Langkau-Herrmann and Sessar-Karpp is similar to that of the Netherlands in that West German women in the 1980s constituted only about a third of all employed persons. Part-time employment is particularly prevalent in West Germany for women. Of all working women, approximately a third work only part-time and two thirds report interrupting their employment for family reasons. Since high level administrative jobs are usually not part-time positions, part-time women employees are almost by definition excluded not only from the high level positions but from the career ladders that lead to these positions. In direct government service, women are not well represented especially at the upper levels. Only 24 percent of all government workers are women. Of these, 36 percent are part-time employees. Only 17 percent of full-time government workers are women. Of all part-time workers, 95 percent are women. While part-time employment and the ability to interrupt employment to bear and care for children is a demand which many in the women's movement have worked to have met, part-time employment and career interruption are not compatible with success in competitive career ladders. The large number of top women administrators in the sample who were unmarried (42 percent) and the larger number who had never had children (70 percent) suggests that Leyenaar's "culture of motherhood" that encourages women to choose between career and family operates in West Germany as it does in the Netherlands.

Finland is unique in the extent to which the government provides employment for women and in the degree of sex segregation that pervades its various levels of government. That 45 percent of the women but only 25 percent of the men work in the public sector suggests that the state, perhaps in response to the tight labor supply, has been successful in attracting women to public employment. Sinkkonen, Hänninen-Salmelin, and Karento describe the ways that women in Finnish public administration are concentrated at the local and municipal levels rather than at the state level. The functions of government, such as health, education, and social services, traditionally female functions, are also concentrated primarily at the local and municipal levels, while state functions involving transportation, finance, law enforcement, and diplomacy are delegated to the state where women are not as well represented either in the bureaucracy or in the legislative bodies.

The size of the federal bureaucracy in the United States and the relatively large numbers of women in top positions (although the percentages may be small) enabled the research in the United States to follow more closely the original research design for the project. The original plan was to interview 12 women in top positions in a traditionally male dominated department such as finance and 12 top women in a department dealing with traditionally female roles in the society such as health, education, or social services. Unlike some other countries, in the United States both the Treasury Department and the Health and Human Services Department had enough women in top positions to accomplish this goal. The United States, the West German, and the Finnish studies unlike the others all included a comparable sample of males that provides a way of checking whether characteristics of the female sample are gender related or due to other factors. The role of women in United States federal government agencies is a particularly skewed one in that women in public service constitute between 57 percent (Agriculture) and 92 percent (Education) of the lowest grade levels GS 1-8 for all thirteen departments, and they compose only between 3 percent (Defense) and 16 percent (Education) of the highest grade levels (GS 16-18 and SES). Roughly speaking, a positive correlation seems to exist between the number of women in the lower levels and number of women in the upper grade levels for any one agency despite the enormous difference in numbers of women in the lower and upper grades.

The findings of the United States study show that the recruitment of women into top positions in the bureaucracy varies significantly according to the function of the agency. Agencies that perform social functions that have traditionally been female roles such as Health and Human Services or Education, tend to recruit larger numbers of women into top positions. Agencies such as Defense, Agriculture, Treasury, and Transportation do not. In addition to presenting comparative information concerning high ranking women in the Treasury and Health and Human Services Departments, the United States data show both male and female top administrators exhibiting open democratic management styles that have traditionally been associated with female administrators.

SUMMARIZING THE SIMILARITIES THAT DESCRIBE WOMEN IN TOP ADMINISTRATIVE POSITIONS

The six countries in this study exhibit some striking similarities with regard to the small numbers of women in top administrative positions, the highly educated backgrounds of these women, the experience of discrimination and the existence of gender related barriers to advancement that these women report in their career histories, and the enormous burden of family, marriage, and child care on women that continues to affect all the women in all the countries. The data generally support, but do not confirm, the notion that women administrators as a whole tend to exhibit a more open, consultative management style in comparison with the typically more authoritarian style of male administrators. The data also support the hypothesis that women as token minorities in most bureaucracies attempt to conform at least to some extent to the existing norms of the organization rather than attempt to make dramatic or heroic efforts to initiate change. Women administrators have confidence in their own abilities, and those who are satisfied with their jobs generally believe that merit (even female merit) is rewarded at least some of the time.

A DISCUSSION OF SOME OF THE MAJOR
DIFFERENCES IN THE COUNTRIES
IN THIS SYMPOSIUM

To assess whether any further useful observations can be drawn from
the comparison of women in top administrative positions in the six countries of this symposium, a discussion of some of their major characteristics
is useful. A discussion of differences in the labor force comes first followed by some information drawn from this study and other aggregate
data sources. Aggregate data for comparative purposes is notoriously in-
accurate. Nevertheless, available aggregate data remain the "best guess"
approximation for purposes such as this one.

WOMEN IN THE LABOR FORCE

Finland, Bulgaria, and the United States all have had significant numbers of women working in the paid labor force for many years. In Finland,
55 percent of all working age women were in the paid labor force as early
as 1900. In Bulgaria, 45 percent of the economically active population
were women in 1946. In the United States, the labor force participation
rate for women was about 19 percent in 1900. This percentage increased
to over 25 percent in 1940 and to over 52 percent by 1985. In Germany,
approximately a third of the labor force has been female since World War
II. The Netherlands is the only European country that does not have a
history of women being very active in the paid labor force. From 1900 to
1960, only about 20 percent of the paid labor force was female. However,
after 1960, this percentage began to rise to about 35 percent where it is
today. In contrast, in India the participation of women in the paid labor
force has declined during the century from 34 percent of the labor force in
1911 to 26 percent by the 1980s. Comparative figures for the early 1980s
are presented in Table 1.

ROLE CONFLICT

The percentage of married women in the paid work force compared
with all women in the paid work force also varies considerably suggesting
that role conflict for working married women is greater in some industrial
cultures than in others. In the United States, most women in the labor
force are married; 56 percent of all women are in paid work, and 52
percent of all women are married and in paid work. In West Germany, the
comparable percentages indicate that 50 percent of all women work, and

Table 1: Comparisons of Labor Force Aggregate Data

	India	USA	Germany	Netherlands	Finland	Bulgaria
% of Paid Labor Force that are women	26	43	39	34	47	43
% of Women who are working for Wages	30	56	50	39	63	67

Joni Seager and Ann Olson. 1986. Women in the World Atlas. N.Y.: Simon and Schuster, 92-99.

33 percent are married and work. In the Netherlands, 39 percent of all women work but only 18 percent of all women work and are married (Seager and Olson 1986, 16).

THE PUBLIC SECTOR

For all the countries in this symposium, the public sector has been extremely important in providing employment for women, especially in recent years. In India in the late 1970s, 53 percent of employed women worked in the public sector—especially in state and local governments. In Finland, 42 percent of the female labor force and only 25 percent of the male labor force were in the public sector in 1983. In both Finland and India, women's public employment has been primarily at the municipal level. In the Netherlands, 49 percent of all employed women were in the public sector in 1981. In the United States, 38 to 42 percent of the jobs on the federal, state, and local levels were held by women in 1980. This distinction between the public and private sectors, of course, is not meaningful in Bulgaria where all employment is public.

OCCUPATIONAL SEX SEGREGATION

Occupational sex segregation characterizes the labor force of all the countries in this study in varying degrees. In India, 83 percent of the female labor force is in agriculture. Of those in the professions, most women are teachers or nurses. In the public sector, most Indian women are clericals, although the number of female administrators, directors, managers, and executives has been increasing somewhat since 1961. The Indian National Employment Service actually classifies jobs into male/female categories. In Finland, the sex segregation of jobs is defined to a substantial degree according to public and private economy cleavages as well as according to the divisions between state and municipal levels of government. Males tend to dominate the private sectors of the economy as well as the state level of the public sector dealing with transportation, roads, rails, highways, police, and the army, while women dominate in the municipalities where the public health, education, and social services functions are administered. The Netherlands, West Germany, and the United States also exhibit continuing job sex segregation. In the Netherlands, one-third of all employed women work in four occupations, while one-third of all employed males work in 14 occupations. Germany is similar to Finland and the Netherlands in that the public sector is a major employer of women. In the United States in the 1980s, 54 percent of all employed women were either in clerical or service jobs. Forty percent of all female workers were employed in only 10 occupations in 1981, including clerical, nursing, retail sales, cashier, waitress, and elementary school teacher occupations. In the public sector of the United States, women dominated the lower but not the middle and upper levels of public administration at both the state and national levels, and were more prevalent in the middle and upper levels in state and local governments than in middle and upper level positions at the national level. Women are more likely to be in leadership positions in occupations that have traditionally been female sex segregated, whether in the public or private sectors.

Bulgaria constitutes a somewhat different case. As Ananieva and Razvigorova note, the socialist revolution has had an enormous impact on Bulgarian women. In 1946, women constituted less than 10 percent of the paid labor force and in 1984, they constituted almost 50 percent of all employed workers. The postwar communist Bulgarian government made a massive attempt to modernize the country and included women as a part of the modernization process. Unlike the women in the other countries in this symposium, Ananieva and Razvigorova report that Bulgarian women are represented in all aspects of the economy — industry, engineering, agriculture, in addition to participating heavily in the service spheres of the economy. Certain professions in Bulgaria continue to exhibit the characteristics of sex segregated occupations. For example, over 70 percent of all teaching and research staffs at all levels are women.

OTHER MAJOR DIFFERENCES

The nations represented in this symposium vary not only in the size of their populations, but also in the organization and ideology of their governments, in the role of the state in the economy of each country, in the history of oppression or colonization, in the rural/urban division of the society, and in religion, to mention a few of the major differences. Table 2 presents some of these contrasts. As a communist country tied in the 1980s to the Soviet bloc, Bulgaria is unique among the other countries in this study. Both Bulgaria and India have recent histories of being con-quered and occupied by foreign invaders: by the Turks and the Germans in the case of Bulgaria, and by the British in the case of India. The govern-ments of both countries have, since 1947-1948, made heroic efforts to modernize primarily agrarian societies. Even today, 83 percent of all working women work in agriculture in India (Seager and Olson 1986, 14), and in Bulgaria, 58 percent of the agricultural labor force are women (Seager and Olson 1986, 41).

The question of religious affiliation in each country and its impact on the situation for women in top administrative positions was factored into the design of this study only as a variable affecting the general socializa-tion of women in that society. Neither the content of the religions nor the content of the dominant government ideologies were within the method-ological framework of this study. The six countries in this symposium, however, do exhibit differences in religious affiliation. Furthermore, the interview and questionnaire data indicate that the way dominant religious philosophies treat women has an impact on more than the socialization of women administrators. It also has an impact on how top women in these societies conduct their administrative duties and the extent of role conflict that they not only experience in their own minds but that their clientele also feel and communicate. These questions deserve further probing in future studies. Table 2 identifies the major religious affiliations in five of the six countries where that information is available.

The six countries also differ in the extent to which they have admitted women to higher education. Table 2 shows that the United States, Bul-garia, and Finland have managed to recruit equal numbers of males and females into higher education at the undergraduate level. At the graduate level, men still dominate. In the United States and in Finland in the early 1980s, women received 32 percent and 24 percent of all PhD degrees respectively (Morgan 1984, 696, 215).

The participation of women in government is another area in which the six countries differ. Five of the countries are democracies while Bulgaria is a socialist state. All have granted women the vote although at different times, and all have allowed women into top governmental positions but have kept the numbers of women at the top very small. India is the only country that has had a female head of government.

Table 2: Some General Characteristics in the 1980s

	India	USA	Germany	Netherland	Finland	Bulgaria
Population in Millions*	635	235	61	14	4.7	4.6
Religious Affiliation in %*	Hindi- 83 Moslem-11 Other- 6	Prot.- 33 Cath.- 22 Other- 5 None - 40	Prot.-49 Cath.-44 Other- 7	Cath.-44 Prot.-24 Other- 8 None- 24	Prot.-93	--
Women in Higher University Education Undergraduates in %*	25 †	53	36	33	49	53
Women in Government						
Cabinet Level Ministers %**	--	15	6	13	18	4
Women in Legislature %**	7	5	11	19	31	22
Women in top levels of Public Administration % ***	11	7	1	5	<1	?

* See Morgan 1984, 215,245,294, 465, and 696. The religious percentages are not comparable as the percentages for the United States and the Netherlands are for the total population, including those who express no religious affiliation, whereas the percentages for the other countries include only those who have expressed a religious affiliation.

† In India, women earned 25 percent of all graduate and undergraduate degrees in 1971. (Morgan 1984, 294).

** See Sivard 1985, 35-37.
*** Data derived from this study. Figures are approximations as definitions of "top level" are difficult to make in six countries on a comparable basis, especially with regard to Bulgaria.

WOMEN IN LEGISLATURES
AND CABINET LEVEL POSTS
IN THE 1980s

One might expect the number of women in higher public administration positions to be related to the number of women in legislatures and in cabinet level posts. Finland has a long history of women's suffrage dating from 1906. Finland was the first country to elect women to parliament in 1907, although even in the 1980s women constituted only 20 percent of the legislative body (Seager and Olson 1986, 30). The country was also one of the first to appoint a woman to a cabinet level post as early as 1926 (Seager and Olson 1986, 30). In the early 1980s, Finland had three women in cabinet level positions. Germany also was relatively early (1919) in granting women the vote, but did not have a female cabinet level member until 1961. In the 1980s, West Germany continued to have only one woman at cabinet level (Seager and Olson 1986, 30). In the German Bundesrat, women held 22 percent of the seats; in the Bundestag, they constituted 10 percent of the body (Morgan 1984, 245). Although parts of India granted women the vote as early as 1921, universal suffrage for all adults over 21 was not achieved until the Constitution of 1950. India had Indira Gandhi as prime minister from 1966-1977. She was reelected in 1980. In the legislature in the early 1980s, women constituted 9 percent of the upper house and 4 percent of the lower house. Two women were ministers of state and two were deputy ministers (Morgan 1984, 294). In the United States, women obtained the vote in 1919. In the 1980s, women constituted 2 percent of the Senate, 5 percent of the House of Representatives, 13 percent of all state legislators, and 9 percent of the judiciary. Three women held cabinet level posts at the national level (Morgan 1984, 697). Bulgaria, with its socialist constitution that provided women the vote in 1947, had women in less than 5 percent of its top level executive and legislative posts in the early 1980s (Seager and Olson 1986, 30). Generally, in all six countries, women are poorly represented in legislatures and in cabinet level posts.

CURRENT PUBLIC POLICIES

Germany, the Netherlands, Bulgaria, the United States, and Finland all have policies that declare women should not be discriminated against, although none of these policies are aggressively enforced. India has a similar provision in its constitution. Finland and Bulgaria have a system of public child care that facilitates women's careers. None of the other countries, however, have any overall public program for child care. West Germany in 1985 instituted a legal leave entitlement for mothers for up to 6 months after childbirth and for either parent for up to five days per year to care for a sick child. In 1986, the German government expanded on this theme and established a "child raising leave" for either parent to care for a child during the year after birth with a job guarantee and monetary allowance. The constitutionality of maternity leave policies in the United States has been challenged in the courts on the grounds of reverse discrimination and left by the Supreme Court to be settled by the states. Some policies continue to mitigate against women's career advancement. In Germany, the practice of having schoolchildren attend school only until noon specifically encourages women to work part-time or drop out of the paid workforce altogether. The West German policy of routinizing part-time work on a regular basis for women makes it possible for many women to engage in paid work; however, it also prevents those women from competing with full-time men for top positions.

Although access to education has improved for women in all six countries, basic socialization practices and attitudes combined with childbearing and childcare responsibilities continue to curb women's career aspirations in all the countries considered here. Indian women are particularly burdened by traditional patterns of behavior and by the inability of the few national public policies favoring greater equality for women to penetrate into rural areas. Affirmative action or positive action programs exist in the United States and in the Netherlands. In the Netherlands, positive discrimination or emancipation policy has attracted considerable attention since 1976 but has brought about few changes. Female respondents in the United States credited affirmative action policies with being important to the advancement of women in public administration.

CONCLUSIONS

The histories, economies, labor markets, governmental institutions, cultures, religions, and political ideologies of the six countries considered here are quite different from one another, yet many of the outcomes for women in public service are similar. Change has occurred in that every country formally declares women to be equal to men. In each country, the public sector has been an important employer of women, and each country has a few women in top administrative positions. Most of these top women have a "token" status as they represent no more than 11 percent of the top administrative ranks in any country. Women are the exceptions while males are the norm. A high level of educational attainment characterizes all the top women administrators. In all the countries, except perhaps Bulgaria where it may be greater, the pool of women engaged in graduate education is less than a third of the total.

The conflict between career and family is apparent in all countries. Women in top administrative positions are less likely to be married, less likely to have children, and if they do have children, they have fewer than their male colleagues or than other females in the society. Countries that provide for childcare, such as Bulgaria and Finland, are small countries with tight labor supplies.

To compare the status of women in high public administrative posts in six countries is one way of comparing how the patriarchy operates with regard to one variable in six countries. The findings of this study suggest that no simple correlations will explain the rich diversity of factors that seem to impinge on this issue. One hypothesis is that the nature of the economy, whether it is primarily agricultural, industrializing, industrial, or service oriented, will set the parameters for women in both the paid and unpaid labor force in different ways. Primarily agricultural societies with strong religious cultures and hierarchical social stratification (like India) may have relatively high levels of female elite representation drawn from the upper classes who bring with them a traditional authority and political acceptability. As the Indian data document, Indian women in top positions experience considerable role conflict because these same traditional values make women's involvement in any public arena, including employment, quite difficult. An industrializing state, such as Bulgaria has been since 1947, may mobilize women, educate them, and place them in high administrative posts because the state needs their skills. Industrial and service oriented economies as they come to need higher levels of education and training to keep pace with technological production and economic crisis also draw women out of the home and into higher education and the job market. In these countries, the pressure for promoting women to high positions seems to come from grassroots movements among women themselves.

Yet, exceptions can be found for every generalization. Each exception tends to raise new questions. Many traditional religious agricultural societies in the Middle East, Africa, or Latin America do not have upper class women in leadership positions, although Latin American countries have had a few. Perhaps this is a feature peculiar to some Asian societies? Might the content of religious beliefs in a country have some bearing on the matter? The Bulgarian example suggests that a strong, centrally directed state can effect a dramatic change in women's educational and employment opportunities especially if labor markets are tight, although it is not clear to what extent Bulgarian women have achieved significant representation in the highest levels of public administration as a consequence of these changes. Does state ideology make a difference? To what extent are East European nations or even the nations of the entire Soviet bloc similar to one another with regard to women in the professional labor force and women in higher education? Are similar pressures extant in the capitalist newly industrializing countries like Japan, Taiwan, or South Korea? And what of the industrial nations? Are not the differences among them with regard to size, laws, and the position of women in top levels of public administration greater than the similarity of economic and political organization?

The interview and questionnaire data for this study support the hypothesis that religious practices and educational opportunities for women are other major variables that help shape the socialization of women in a society. Most major religions advocate a domestic, if not a sequestered, role for women. In states with strong religious traditions and institutions, a female administrator who may escape being deterred by religious values in her own socialization and advancement still lives and works in a society where these values persist. If the dominant religious values place women squarely in the home and not elsewhere, the female administrator must deal with the resulting role conflict on an everyday basis.

Higher education for women is perhaps the only prerequisite for a top position in public administration in all countries, yet even here the data support no indication of a constant correlation or relationship with the percentages of women in higher public administrative positions. The data suggest precisely the opposite. India has half the percentage of women obtaining higher degrees in comparison with the United States or Finland, and yet India seems to have a larger percentage of women in the Indian Administrative Service, the elite Indian civil service.

The above comparisons show that no simple correlations emerge from the data to explain in a general way either why women have been able to obtain positions in higher administration in some countries or why they have not. Each country demands its own story. The complexity of the issue and the small number of countries in this study may well be reasons for this. Only if very strong correlations were extant would they emerge in a study of only six countries. Weak linkage between a host of variables seems to define the situation in most cases. Another explanation may be the one mentioned in the introduction. The similarities that appear to exist may well be generated by a multitude of quite different conditions.

POLICIES AND STRATEGIES

If the above analysis is correct and the advance of women in public administration is weakly dependent on a host of variables, then what prospects are there for positive change and what strategies should those pursue who would like to improve the global position of women in public administration? Since the problem seems to be multi-causal and integrally related to the specific society, the strategies have to be designed accordingly to keep the pressure on in a host of different ways with particular attention to the peculiarities of each country and culture. Strategies aimed at consciousness raising, ideological, institutional, and symbolic change are essential. Working to change women's position in the labor force, working to improve education and higher education for women, working to change laws that oppress and limit women, working to reduce role conflict for top administrative women, working in the international women's movement to influence bureaucracies, and working within bureaucracies themselves also are important strategies. Getting more women into top administrative offices will accomplish other important objectives. Once women obtain a critical mass of at least 20 percent of top administrative jobs and are not required to behave as "tokens," the overall mix of management styles should change. The recruitment and promotion of women should become easier. Bureaucracies may not be on the cutting edge of social change; however, once change does occur within them, they can institutionalize the change and help make it a permanent part of the social fabric.

REFERENCES

Brekke, Toril et. al. 1985 *Women: A World Report.* London: Methuen London Ltd.

Farley, Jennie, ed. 1985. *Women Workers in Fifteen Countries* Ithaca, N.Y.: Cornell University Press.

Iglitzin and Ross. 1986 (p. 1).

Jacquette, Jane S. 1989. *The Women's Movement in Latin America: Feminism and the Transition to Democracy* Winchester Mass: Unwin Hyman.

Joekes, Susan. 1987. *Women in the World Economy: An INSTRAW Study* New York: Oxford University Press.

Lovenduski, Joni. 1986. *Women and European Politics: Contemporary Feminism and Public Policy.* Amherst, Mass: U. of Massachusetts Press.

Morgan, Robin, ed. 1984. *Sisterhood is Global.* Garden City, N.Y.: Anchor Press/Doubleday.

Randall, Vicky. 1987. *Women and Politics: An International Perspective.* Chicago: University of Chicago Press.

Seager, Joni, and Ann Olson. 1986. *Women in the World Atlas.* N.Y.: Simon & Schuster.

Sivard, Ruth Leger. 1985. *Women: A World Survey.* Washington, D.C.: World Priorities.

About the Contributors

NORA ANANIEVA is Professor of Government at the Institute for Modern Social Sciences at the University of Sofia in Sofia, Bulgaria.

JEANNE MARIE COL is Associate Professor of Public Administration at Sangamon State University. She is author of "Guidelines for Policy Development for Increased Participation of Women in Public Management." Currently she is serving as Special Technical Advisor in Public Administration in the United Nations Secretariat.

EVA HÄNNINEN-SALMELIN is a Research Manager and a Trainer of the International Women's Management Institute in Tampere, Finland. She holds a Master of Arts in Political Science and has been a researcher and acting lecturer at the University of Tampere. Her research interests include women in management, women in government services, and women in power.

MONIKA LANGKAU-HERRMANN is Head of the Department of Women's Politics in the Friedrich-Ebert Foundation. Her research interests concern labour market problems, women in politics, private industry, and public services.

MONIQUE LEYENAAR is Professor of Political Science at the University of Nijmegen in the Netherlands. She is serving as a consultant to the Netherlands government on the issue of how to increase the participation of women in government and politics. Her current research interests concern local democracy and local politics.

EVKA RAZVIGOROVA is Deputy Director of the National Research and Training Institute for Public Administration in Sofia, Bulgaria.

ELLEN SESSAR-KARPP is Director of the Women's Technical Center in Hamburg, Germany. Her research interests concern women in technology, women in top positions, and the role of women in the European market.

NIROJ SINHA is the Director of the Centre for Women's Development Studies in Bihar, India. She is currently studying the organization of

133

women's groups and the mobilization and development of women on the village level in Bihar.

SIRKKA SINKKONEN is a Professor of Health and Nursing Administration at the University of Kuopio, Finland. She is the author of *Marital Happiness in the Modern and Traditional Marriage* (Kuopio 1975), *Nursing Science* (Kuopio 1983), and various articles on the organization of the health services, political science and public administration, and women and politics, including "Women in Local Politics" in *Unfinished Democracy: Women in Nordic Politics*, eds. Elina Haavio-Mannila et al. (Pergamon Press 1985). She has participated in international work through the World Health Organization and the Executive Council of the International Political Association.

HEM LATA SWARUP is Ex-Vice Chancellor of Kanpur University in Kanpur, India. Her current research interests focus on women, environmental policy and peace.

Index

teamwork approach, 100

unemployment rate, India, 15-16
United States
  civil servants, 88-89,92,93,95
  federal administrative system,
    87-88,92
  labor history, 85-88
  laws governing women's
    employment, 87-88,92
  political appointees, 88-89,92,93,
    95
  women in labor force, 85-88,
    89-91t
  women in top positions, 85-109,
    119-120

wage discrimination, India, 15
wife/mother role, 21,28-29,118,119,
  121,128
women
  emancipation, 31-32,50-53
  inferior position of, 51
  motivation to work, 33,117-18
  socioeconomic improvements for,
    13-14
  status in India, 13,116-17
women in labor force, 121
  Bulgaria, 32-34
  Finland, 69-70
  India, 14-16
  · the Netherlands, 41-43,118
  United States, 85-88,89-91t,92
  West Germany, 55,118-19
women in top positions
  age, 76,77t,114-15
  aggressive methods of, 61
  attitude towards, 47
  barriers to, 27-29,66-67,80-81,
    115
  Bulgaria, 31-40,117-18
  career choices, 25,37-38,95,97

career development, 35-37,38,
  46-47,52-53
career histories, 25,78-79,93,95,
  108-109
career/family conflict, 21,28-29,
  39,118,119,121,128
case studies, 16-29,34-40,45-49,
  76-82,92-107
discrimination, 25-26,27-28,48,61
education, 24-25,52,59-60,76-77,
  78t,113,124,127-28,129
family background, 23,24,27,80,
  93,113,114
family interference, 29
family life, 103-104
family size, 24,81-82,103-104,
  114,128
feminism and, 48,105-106,107,
  108
Finland, 69-82,119
hierarchical structures and, 64,67
income, 19-21,43-44,45-46
India, 13-29,116-17
job responsibilities, 98
job satisfaction, 37-38,62,79-80,
  98-99
management style, 47-48,62-64,
  99-101,115-16,120
marriage, 23,59,81,114
mentoring activities, 65-66
the Netherlands, 41-53,118
numbers of, 17-18,25,43-45,
  112-13
political pressures, 26
professional development, 60-61
promotion, 19-21,26-27,38,56-57,
  60-61,66,80,104-105
in public sector, 55-58,69-70,122
recruitment, 18,19t,52,61,66
religious affiliation, 24,124,
  128-29
resignation reasons, 49t
role conflicts, 21,28-29,39,118,
  119,121,128